NIXON'S INHERITANCE:
A DRUNKEN ECONOMY

NIXON'S INHERITANCE:

A DRUNKEN ECONOMY

by

RICHARD A. BEACH

Library of Congress Catalog No. 72-76585

Copyright 1972 by Richard A. Beach

Libra Publishers, Inc.
391 Willets Road
Roslyn Heights, N.Y. 11577

Manufactured in the United States of America

To

Margaret Anne Beach

"Nothing can be more deplorable than an inheritance of triumphant wrong."

Lord Palmerston (1784-1865)

TABLE OF CONTENTS

Chapter   Page

PREFACE

Politics and economics have been wed for many years. It has seldom been a comfortable marriage. Which partner is responsible for what and which deserves the castigation or acclaim has been a bewilderment to most who have tried to judge them fairly.

In a democracy, the ultimate determination of economic policies rests with the electorate. Unfortunately we are not all economists, and more significantly, the general level of understanding of economics leaves enormous room for improvements. And the diversity of opinion among the scholars compounds the problem of raising the level of understanding. In even the most sincere efforts, a heavy dose of political prejudice is virtually unavoidable and I make no claims to having succeeded in avoiding it here. The search for truth becomes a veritable maze as facts about economics are distorted and disseminated to serve special interests.

In spite of this we are frequently called upon to judge. Hopefully the disclosures and perspectives that follow will be helpful the next time you stand in judgment of the participants of this unfortunate marriage.

I wish to express my gratitude to my friend Dr. Frederick L. Thomsen, a consulting economist, for his help and suggestions—many of which are reflected in this book. To J. Allan Rudolph, who has served as a sounding board and has been generous in challenging the ideas developed here. And to my wife Margaret who has been an inordinately encouraging as well as tactful critic.

Richard A. Beach

NIXON'S INHERITANCE:

A DRUNKEN ECONOMY

Chapter I

THE HANGOVER

In the bright light of the morning after, without the artificially induced euphoria, realities look harsh. The night before, with the free flowing stimulant, money, the economic world looked beautiful. The "economic body" suffers the pains of adjustment when regaining balance after imbibing excessive stimulants. Our experience in the sixties was one of an economy going from recession to boom. This was a jerky, halting, accelerating, decelerating experience—one that went from high unemployment to low unemployment, from a low utilization of our plant equipment and low profitability, to a high utilization and high profitability. As a result, it was difficult for the businessman, the consumer, and the government to discern which portion of their advancement was attributable to the recovery from a depressed situation and which portion was attributable to the move into the area of excesses—the unsustainable boom-time levels of business.

For the consumer, the early stages of recovery find him with larger paychecks and with more purchasing power. The later phase of boom-time excesses finds him with more dollar income, but generally with no greater or even less real income. In the early stages his income rises faster than prices. In the latter stages, while income is rising, the cost of living rises as fast or faster, negating the dollar income advancement. After a period, "overtime" work is taken for granted, even though it is an abnormal condition. Consumption patterns are adjusted to the overtime and newer and larger consumer debts are incurred, relying on this abnormally increased income. The return to regular hours without overtime

3

becomes by comparison, a personal recession for these people. The same can be said for the commission salesman as he begins to take the exaggerated level of sales for granted. The strained financial condition of these people during the adjustment is made even more severe by the "lagging" nature of inflation. The forces of inflation tend to persist, even after the pulling forces of excessive demand have subsided, thus straining even farther their already difficult financial situation.

For the businessman, a long expansion is a glorious experience. More business and the increasing efficiencies resulting from a better use of his plant equipment would be nice enough. But there are other facets that make it delightful. The business seems to be operating at capacity. He can commonly raise the prices for his products faster than he must raise wages. In the early stages of the economic expansion—the recovery phase—his profits rise rapidly as compared to the preceding period of under-utilization of his business capabilities. In the latter phase of his expansion (the unsustainable boom-time excesses) the profits continue to rise, but for a quite different reason. It is, as we have mentioned, that his prices are able to rise faster than his labor and other costs.

A factor enhancing the businessman's joy during the expansion is that as consumer incomes rise, consumer patterns change or broaden. Areas of business activities that previously were marginal, frequently become very profitable during such a period. Consumption of those goods and services that were reserved for a few become available to larger and larger numbers as incomes increase. The move toward the greater consumption of luxury items and services has a disproportionate impact upon some companies. Their business expansion, because of the change of boom-time consumer patterns, is far greater than the average for the economy as a whole. Manufacturers and distributors of private yachts and airplanes find business fantastic when compared to a period of recession, or expansion without excesses. A long list of businesses so affected could be compiled. All have enjoyed a bet-

4

ter than average expansion that is attributable to the broadening or changing consumer patterns.

As a result a larger number of glamour industries developed. The greater amount of personal income spent "eating out," for example, was a major factor and great stimulus for the "franchise" food and restaurant business. More money available for recreation revitalized the moving picture industry. It was also responsible for the proliferation of bowling alleys. The spectacular raises sparked the development of all manner of recreation industries and even the toy industry witnessed a great acceleration because of the money available for such luxuries. Residential construction is influenced as people feel they have the means to maintain two or more homes. Also, the growing number of highly paid young people has been responsible for the construction of whole apartment complexes devoted to the whims of young singles.

The booming stock market exemplified the economic excesses. The wide acceptance of stock prices that rise to multiples of fifty or one hundred times earnings is a clear manifestation of how pervasive the optimism can become. In such an intoxicating atmosphere very few remain rational. The great profit gains resulting from the changing consumer patterns become a contagious lure. Imaginations are turned loose without limits. Virtually every such period in history has been accompanied by the financial innovators. In this period, high stock prices motivated the financial wizardry of the conglomerates and facilitated their financial manipulations.

The architects of the "conglomorate" would combine businesses through financial arrangements or rearrangements of stock, preferred stock, convertible preferred stock and debentures and convertible debentures, exploiting the then existing corporate income tax structure in order to show higher earnings. Such a mirror trick could be highly rewarding for the stock manipulators.

The "swinger" mutual fund was another quite natural outgrowth of the changing consumer and investment pattern.

5

The "get rich quick" atmosphere captured the fancy of the small investors, many of whom had money available for investment for the first time. The investing "intermediaries," the mutual funds, provided the greedy and reckless a medium of investment, or more appropriately, of speculation. The pervasiveness of this demand is demonstrated by the fact that the largest portion of mutual fund sales during the late sixties was in those funds offering the most aggressive investment policies.

In the year 1969 interest rates were so high as to find precedent only in the years preceding the Civil War. This demand for credit might be compared to the drunk who is seeking another drink after the normal closing hours of the bars. His demand for a drink and his view of the benefits he will derive from it make him willing to pay exorbitant prices. Borrowers envision great benefits from their use of the borrowed funds—influenced by the inebriated perspective of boom-time projections. Lenders, viewing the inflation costs, demand higher and higher prices for the use of their money.

Businessmen and consumers, like drunks, often tend to "imbibe" to excess. For the businessman, an area of profitability will draw more and more units of business until too many are allocated to that particular economic need. This encourages the consumers, deriving their income from such expanding enterprises, to overshot their long-run consumption potential or ability.

Regardless of how ludicrous the excesses are in retrospect, at the time they are occuring, they are beautiful, glorious, and appear natural and normal. For those who would seek to avoid these excesses, solutions requiring that the excesses be recognized by consumers, businessmen, government or employees are doomed to failure. The ability and the will of people in general to forego the pleasures of booming prosperity are not reliable inhibitors. Drunks cannot be expected to "swear off" while on a "bender." Only in the subsequent hours of discomfort and sobriety is a course of temperance likely to be adopted. Such a course, to be successful, will

6

generally entail strict, reliable rules that are simple enough
to prevail in moments of temptation. They might be, for example, for the drunk, complete abstention, or maybe a two
drink limit. Since government, too, is run by people with
these same very human inadequacies of judgment, economic
stability will have to come from an economic environment
that does not rely upon the exercising of human judgment
from moment to moment under all conditions. As we have
pointed out, human judgment is by its very nature, easily misled and thereby destabilizing.

THE MORNING AFTER

Our simile extends easily. Drunks are almost universally
aware of the fact that the severity of the discomforts of the
"morning after" are proportional to the degree of excesses of
the night before. In economics, excesses can be defined as
such only on measuring the magnitude in terms of the disruption they cause. Without disruption, there are no excesses.
An inflationary boom requires an ever-increasing supply
of money. The further this situation moves from a sustainable long-run rate, the more difficult the adjustment will be
when moving back toward that rate. Essentially, the pain of
adjustment is a matter of comparisons. The inflated boom-
time profits, the inflated personal income, the inflated stock
prices, the inflated real estate prices, and not the least, the
inflated expectations, make that which preceded them and
that which follows look poor and unglamorous. Levels of economic activity at a time prior to the boom may have been
generally satisfactory, while after the boom, similar levels become very depressing. Absolute economic measurements during a recession year may compare very favorably with the
period just two or three years previous, omitting the boom
year or years from the comparison. Total employment, total
personal income, total corporate profits, total output, and the
gross national product may very well exceed the figures of

the pre-boom period. One might ask then, "Why do people become so depressed when conditions aren't so bad after all?" For some, the statistics are meaningless because for them the recession is a personal disaster. Their small business didn't decline ten percent, it went bankrupt. For some individuals, employment doesn't drop four percent, it drops one-hundred percent. For many who are not affected, knowledge of the affected is disquieting, if not depressing. Perhaps an even more pervasive effect is the shattering of dreams and the demolishing of castles in the sky, resulting from the gross over-enthusiasm and distorted expectations for their business enterprises or stock investments.

One of the nation's indexes of discomfort during a recession is an economic statistic called "unemployment." In 1946, Congress, evidently feeling confident of its economic power, ascribed to itself the responsibility for maintaining "full employment." This statistic has become a political obsession. The party in power points to this statistic when it is favorable, citing it as a measure of its good administration. When the unemployment figure is comparatively high, the party out of power cites it as a measure of how poorly the administration is performing. Somehow, the nation has assured the prejudice that everybody who seeks employment is entitled to employment, regardless of their skills, abilities, willingness to work, or desire to change jobs. This is a remarkable bit of logic, but we as a nation have been stuck with it for many years.

This nation has a very broad and manifold system of distributing income. This income comes from wages, rent, royalties, dividends, interest, insurance, social security, pensions, disability programs, welfare, subsidies, gifts, and all manner of family sharing. These sources of dollar income do not take into account the real income resulting from people doing for themselves, such as sewing, housework, home maintenance, vegetable gardening, and for some, hunting and fishing. These diverse sources of real income for many thousands

8

make temporary unemployment an inconvenience rather than a true hardship.

For many, however, a trend away from "*overfull employment*" is more inconvenient than rising unemployment is for others. In the late sixties, we witnessed a period when demands for labor were so excessive that overtime was the rule rather than the exception for millions.

Some employees who had reached retirement age were encouraged to continue working because of the excess demands on their businesses. Housewives, who might otherwise not have been employed, were encouraged to work in family businesses, for friends who knew of their abilities, or because of the easy availability of work. The ready availability of work to teenagers whose income is spent on luxury and frivolity drew thousands of them into the work force. Several reports were that construction contractors and people of the building trades were in such demand that they were able to receive time-and-a-half and double-time for their regular working hours. Employers were willing to pay in order to lure them away from other construction jobs. Normalcy, when compared to these "*overful employment*" conditions, appears as a depression, as sobriety often compares unfavorably to the "highs" of inebriation.

The real squeeze on personal income is not from unemployment, or the lack of benefits from over-employment; it comes from inflation. Families whose dollar income is unchanged find themselves with less and less buying power. This is far broader in its effect than is unemployment. For those whose dollar income has declined as a result of a recession, the situation is made only more harsh by the inflation. Unfortunately, one of the hangovers of an inflationary boom is the inflation. There is a lag effect to the forces of inflation which cause it to persist for some time after the boom time pressures have passed.

The consumer debt commitments made during the optimism of the boom period continue afterward. While the costs of these commitments generally do not rise, they have a priority over most others. The rising costs of other items in the family budget force a change in consumption patterns, affecting most greatly the items of lowest priority. As we have pointed out, during the expansion phase, many companies had spectacular growth as a result of changing consumer patterns. Inversely, a revision of consumer patterns during an economic adjustment affects businesses greatly. Those businesses which provide the products or services people can most easily forego are the most adversely affected during an adjustment.

Business profits are very highly sensitive to economic activity, particularly recession. After the volume of business has failed to expand or even has contracted, the costs of business continues to rise. Large corporations make commitments to increase wages for three years in advance and despite the fact that gross revenues are declining, labor costs continue to rise. Businessmen in a period of optimism often decide to maximize the growth of business earnings by borrowing money instead of selling stock to raise capital. They find that the financial leverage which was to work so wonderfully in their favor works effectively to their detriment during a recession. A more acute pain resulting from the squeeze in corporate earnings is the decline of stock prices. The practice of calculating one's net worth by multiplying the last price at which the stock traded by the number of shares one holds can be just as depressing after the market has fallen as it was exhilerating during the boom. Persons experiencing no decline in real income can spend day after day in deep dejection after calculating their net worth. For those whose over-optimism led them to borrow money in order to add to their stock holdings, "paper losses" can quickly turn into "realized losses" and do so quite involuntarily. For these people, the anxieties caused by the anticipation of a "call" from their banker or broker asking for money or more collateral can be worse than any hangover. Stockholders have their moments of depression in concert with other depressed

10

elements in the economy. In contrast, bondholders witness their depression during a period of booming prosperity. As inflation increases, interest rates increase, and as a result, bond prices decline. During 1969, for example, in the midst of booming prosperity, some bond prices declined to forty or fifty percent of their values some three years earlier. While few concern themselves with the miserable plight of the bondholder during the boom years, few also notice their recovery in the leaner years. As the inflationary pressures decline, interest rates decline. The inevitable consequences are higher bond prices. In any event, the convulsions in the bond markets during the late 1960's were without precedent.

HOW DEPRESSING

The adjustments necessary in order to change inflationary to non-inflationary psychology implicitly contain some very depressing elements. In order to tame the wild and unbridled optimism of the boom, attitudes must be forcibly modified. Abandonment of a pleasant state of mind comes about with great reluctance. Because the length or duration of the most recent expansion was so protracted, these overly optimistic attitudes became very durable. The amount of restraint of the economy necessary, therefore, to force the revision of these attitudes became substantially greater than if the holders of these attitudes were more timid. Axiomatically, however, such timidity comes from the recent experience of a threat to security. The longer the expansion is in force, the more the memories of the economic pitfalls become dim. For many, economic experiences are new and the protracted expansion nurtures an ever larger group which is without any inhibiting remembrances of lessening prosperity.

Consumers, businessmen, politicians, and for that matter, many economists tend to base their forecast upon their most recent experience. The reasoning behind this is rather elusive. Apart from the question of whether it is correct or incorrect, it evidently is a characteristic of human nature, and therefore must be accepted as such. This phenomenon causes businessmen to forecast economic expansion after the expansion has terminated. It causes them to forecast recession, even after the recovery phase is in force. They are correct only after the trend has continued long enough for the most recent experience to be valid in extension.

The post-World War II experience was such as to make businessmen and investors very bold. In the fifties, with memories of depression days still vivid, entrepreneurs became very fearful at the slightest down turn in economic activity. On the other hand, after a decade of uninterrupted economic expansion, and relying on the post-war experience of very modest and brief recessions, businessmen and investors became very bold. Their inclinations were to look beyond what they anticipated as being a very short period of business slack. As a result, expansion programs were not as quickly abandoned. The quick nervous nature of the stock market has been largely replaced with a confident air of tolerance, endurance and patience. Such attitudes tend to lengthen the "lag" and impede the quickness with which the economic participants respond to the economic trend. Human nature is reliable, however, and, while the lag can be lengthened, this extension can be measured in mere months. The more pronounced a new trend becomes, the more followers it lures. Pessimism is as contagious as optimism. It too can infect vast populations in a very short period of time. The discomforts from such slack become excruciating when the trend is projected into the future. In spite of the fact that the "bad times" are not really bad compared to a substantially earlier period, they are very painful when compared to the most recent past.

In such slack times, persons who engage in poor business practices commonly fail. Such a period becomes a time of "survival of the fittest." The most efficient and productive survive in business. The unsound financial manipulations common to boom times are most likely to flounder in a slack

12

time. Business judgments tend to overshoot their mark. Such miscalulations are greatest during boom times. Many business judgments that would have been wrong in normal times are passable in boom times. This has a cumulative effect. Those that were spared temporarily by the boom conditions are added to the normal business failures, and the number of business failures seems inflated.

For the individuals severely affected by hard times, return to the old ways of reckless abandon is more difficult, if not impossible. Similarly, those areas of business most harshly affected by an economic recession are slow to return to the old exuberance. The stock market may fit this category. Long depressed markets are slow to recover, while quickly depressed markets tend to recover just as quickly.

There tends to be a lag in the response of the state and local governments to economic decline as well. Perhaps this is because only when an election reveals that the people have changed their attitude does local government adopt the new attitude. Also, there tends to be some lag in the effect of the new economic conditions on the finances of local government.

People tend to forecast optimistically and pessimistically with equal skill. In good times the estimates are boundless, while in bad times doom and gloom are unbridled. Since the pain of a recession is such only in comparison to the "highs" of the preceding boom, the long view yields a much more valid prospective.

THERE'S HOPE

During a period of illness, one may become so involved with discomforts that a good overall perspective is temporarily lost. Our response to economic ills has been similar to our response to personal illness. We rush to treat the painful symptoms. While they are not the cause of the illness, at least if they disappear, the illness won't seem so bad. History

13

has shown that hurried remedies for economic illnesses have resulted in post-illness side effects. The side effects take the form of ill-conceived programs that seem to hang on long after the illness is gone. Frequently, the rash "inflation" results from exessive doses of money and credit. To continue our analogy with the alcoholic, when the drunk wakes up with his terrible hangover he commonly seeks an "eye opener" or a little "hair of the dog that bit him." This is to say, he turns back to the booze as a cure for his hangover. Our "economic planners" have very frequently chosen similar solutions. They have returned time and time again to the booze —money and credit—to cure the symptoms of the recession. And economic alcoholism continues. There is hope, however, for the economic body just as there is for our physical body. If we endure the pain and discomforts of the hangover and permit the body to regain its chemical balance and general health, we can live happy, well-balanced and productive lives. The economy, too, can live without artificial stimulants.

The economy has demonstrated over a period of three-quarters of a century the ability to grow at the rate of three and one-half to four percent, compounded annually. It has done this in spite of our transgressions. While too much money is bad for the economy, too little is equally bad. But, despite periods when the economy was starved for sufficient money on which to operate, the overall growth rate in the long run continued at three and one-half to four percent per year. We should take confidence in this great resiliance. This rate of growth has transcended world wars and depressions. The record shows it to be so durable that not only should we take confidence in the belief that it will continue at approximately that rate, but we should make whatever psychological and emotional adjustments that are necessary to accept that rate and little more.

Economic growth is infinite, and its potentials are far beyond the vision of the most imaginative. The economic achievements of each succeeding generation will be even more unbelievable than it was before, because our achievements are accumulating in a geometric progression. These remarkable feats will be accomplished regardless of how we deal with the very temporary discomforts resulting from economic excesses.

Frequently, people think of increased unemployment in terms of individuals being continuously unemployed. The fact is, however, that unemployment is primarily a measurement of people who are between jobs. Increased unemployment figures mean that the period it takes the unemployed to find new work lengthens. This measurement is in days or weeks, and does not mean, as some would believe, that most of these people become totally unable to find employment.

The jerky, halting stop-and-go economic policy of the federal government has caused dislocation and disruption for many families. As the government has vacillated between policies of stimulation and restraint, accenting one phase of economic activity or another, moving from defense to home building, to space, to pollution, people are lured into one field and then another, only to find themselves subsequently unemployed. Instability in Washington means instability for millions of American families.

There is indeed hope. If investors, businessmen and wage earners decide collectively or individually that they do not like the pain and discomfort of an economic hangover or adjustment, all they need do is to resolve to stay off the booze—elect representatives to go to Washington who are dedicated to avoidance of excessive stimulation of the economy through too rapid expansion of the money supply. Failure simply means more hangovers in the future—more inflation, higher interest rates, vacillating earnings, periods of higher unemployment, and general economic insecurity.

Chapter II

AN EYE OPENER

A monstrous error of our times is the association of the Administration with the level of economic activity at each point in time. If the relative level seems high, the administration is judged to be good, and if the level is lower, it is judged to be poor. The fact is that the level of economic activity over the long run tends to expand regardless of who is in power. No administration deserves credit for this phenomenon. On the other hand, any government acting to achieve a rapid rise in the level of economic activity can do so by generating large deficits that directly or indirectly force the rapid expansion of the money supply. If such expansion proved to be unsustainable and only a short-lived distortion which created an inflationary spiral and other imbalances, what acclaim would such an administration deserve. On the other hand, the Nixon administration which inherited an economy with spiraling inflation, a warped level of capital goods production, a stockmarket bubbling with speculation and a credit-structured spending binge, can hardly be castigated for the eventual adjustment.

It is obvious, therefore, that an administration cannot be judged on its economic policies by examining the short-run level of economic activity. Such a judgment can rest only on long-run results. Inasmuch as economic advancement is infinite, there is no goal toward which to race. Thus, good economic policies are those which foster a rate of economic expansion that is sustainable in the long run, that is relatively stable, and compares favorably with previous long-run per-

17

formances as well as with the long-run performances of other nations.

Should our experience with money and credit during the decade of the sixties be compared with a drunken binge? In order to make such a comparison, we would have to show the manner in which the participants arrived at their uneviable states of inebriation.

The drunkard commonly begins drinking by experimenting with various alcoholic beverages but he exercises considerable caution. In a similar manner, we as an economy, once sampled cautiously the different forms of credit available. This was true for the individual and for society as a whole. Thirty years ago our country was quite wary of the manifold credit innovations. Much in the way individuals become conditioned to and familiar with inebriation, our society became more and more at ease with a larger and larger debt burden.

There are drinkers who go off the deep end, seeking escape from reality in alcohol until finally they drink only in order to delay the arrival of the inevitable hangover. In a similar fashion, many families reached total insolvency by trying to satisfy bill collectors with additional borrowed money. Society, too, prolonged the economic inebriation and postponed the hangover of economic adjustment through the rapid expansion of the federal debt and a consequent rapid expansion of the money supply.

In the case of the drunk, substantial inbalances occur in his body chemistry and metabolism. In the economic organism, substantial imbalances also occur. These, however, become manfest in the form of inflation, high interest rates, speculation in real estate, securities and commodities markets, and a deterioration in foreign trade balances. In truth, nations, individuals and drunks whether they indulge themselves with money credit or with alcohol, only make their eventual adjustment more difficult by delaying that inevitable "headache."

During our economic binge, the "Sorry, Sam, you've had

18

enough" boys have been as popular and persuasive as a stubborn bartender is to a drunk. The euphoric obliviousness seemed to pervade both the alcoholic and the credit drunks. The hope, of course, lies in the subsequently more sober period when reason has an assist from the heavy hand of a hangover. If at that time, such a commitment to the more temperate use of money and credit is not forthcoming, we as a nation may stand condemned to a gross instability in our economy that can be compared with the personal misfortunes of an alcoholic.

The decade of the sixties was characterized, economically speaking, by a rapid and almost uninterrupted rise of nearly all economic indicators. A dominating factor in this expansion has been money and credit. During this period, we experienced the aggressive and exhaustive exploitation of money, the consequence of which generated the most phenomenal boom in this nation's history. So vast have been the changes in the general attitude toward credit that they have worked to transform our political philosophy and even helped, some believe, to weaken our spiritual fiber. As a nation, we became so obsessed with economic boom that almost no price was too high to pay for the hope of retaining it. This blinded us to the conditions that warn us that such a course was unsustainable. Concern for the future security of individual freedom and the welfare of the generations to follow has taken a back seat to our immediate self-indulgent materialism.

People often restrict their concern to consumer credit because they are closest to it. Nearly everyone sees situations in which the application of credit makes little sense and is a source of family or personal anxiety. I shall therefore try to focus on the broad spectrum of money and credit and their effects on the economy—dealing with the major categories and the ways in which they are interdependent. It is within this framework of credit that I wish to paint a picture of our economy as it appeared when President Nixon took office in 1969.

A couple of lines from Fredrick Duerrenmatt's play, "The Visit," might help set the stage: The Burgomaster who is displaying an affluence beyond his known means, when challenged, asks: "Is prosperity a crime?" Shill, whose own wellbeing is at stake retorts, "That depends how you pay for it."[1]

One would think that the boom would have been apparent to all. The long duration of this economic expansion has, however, encompassed most of the adult life of a majority of our citizens. This expansion has been so extended that many have come to take it for granted and to believe that it is the "normal" way economic systems function. Only in retrospect is it readily apparent how inebriated we really were.

Few indeed had escaped personal contact with affluence. For those who failed to enjoy an awareness from their personal experience, all manner of communications were enlisted to spread the glad tidings. The development of economic accounting methods and a broadening familiarity with them have assisted immensely our sensitivity of economic fluctuations. Knowledge of minute changes in indexes and statistics can be forced upon people who would otherwise have no contact with or interest in them. Such "improving" statistics as the "Gross National Product," Disposable Income," "Cost Of Living Index," "The Total Number Employed," and "The Percentage of Unemployed" were disseminated through the news media to nearly every American home. Politicians and businessmen have a vested interested in this purveyance. The preponderance of good economic news has become a popular tool of politicians who would associate themselves with it. The favorable news has become a catalyst for creating optimism, a vital element of successful politics.

The money-nurtured boom is evident everywhere. An awesome experience today is the return to a city after a five or six year absence. The changes are often so extensive that one can feel lost in an area that was once very familiar. New expressways, massive shopping centers, schools, motels, restaurants, and large apartment and office buildings have completely transformed metropolitan areas. Capital outlays on new service stations, churches, and all manner of small enterprises have changed the appearance of most city arteries in recent years. There is hardly a commercial bank which does not operate in a new building or in one that has been completely remodeled in the last decade. The great debt-financed investments of municipal and local governments in such things as fire stations, libraries and office buildings are easily seen. Other, often greater investments, are not as visible. The extensively improved and expanded sewer, water and gas systems are either buried beneath the ground or concealed from view of the casual observer.

Far more subtle manifestations of the economic distortion is the inflation which reduced the savings of our thrifty citizens about one-fourth in a six-year period. Disruptions in international trade and the devaluation of the dollar in terms of foreign goods are products of the boom. Between the vast amounts of over-time worked by American labor and the speculative binge that occurred in the stock market, few families were untouched by the boom.

A SOBER PERSPECTIVE

By the end of 1968, hardly a publication, when dealing with the level of economic activity, omitted the word "boom." The word, however, carries with it the ominous implication of "bust." It commonly implies that the nature of the prosperity is such that it cannot be sustained and that there exists a formidable threat to its existence. The optimistic belief that we had developed a perpetually accelerating prosperity under the label of "New Economics," allowed journalists greater abandon in applying the word "boom." The serious vendors of confidence—the politicians and businessmen—still find the word objectionable. They

21

prefer the term "growth." "Growth" is a pleasing word and does not have the unpleasant implications. In defining economic growth, Professor Simon Kuznets said, " . . . the increase must be sustained over a period long enough to reflect more than a cyclical expansion . . . or some other transient rise.[2] "Boom," on the other hand, is defined in the Encyclopedia of Banking and Finance as "a movement characterized by industrial and commercial activity, rising prices, and sentimentally by optimism and speculative enthusiasm until unwarranted high levels are reached culminating in a reaction.[3] Professor Alvin H. Hanson wrote, "Every boom represents a distortion away from equilibrium or balanced condition. This distortion consists essentially of an unmaintainable rate of capital formation."[4]

The conditions set forth in these definitions of boom were met in 1968. The long duration of the expansion led many to believe that what we had experienced was pure growth. There are many elements of growth that are present in the economy in good times and bad. Throughout the great depression, population continued to grow, invention continued and improvements in our efficiency, knowledge and total human ability continued. These forces have worked well throughout the expansion. This expansion lasted so long because of a continual acceleration in the expansion of the money supply—promoted by the implementation of an economic philosophy of continuing federal deficits during a period of full employment which had been disarmingly labelled the "New Economics." From these latest developments, an idea was promoted that through federal credit—or debt, if you prefer—perpetual boom, and the permanent avoidance of economic adjustment was possible.

If one were to select a few examples of the genius of this country, it would be hard to overlook the schemes, devices, and instruments conceived to generate debt. So successful have been these "debt-generators" that the rate of debt creation in some categories has been so great, it is little wonder disequilibrium occurred. To the extent then that this credit contributed to the economic expansion and cannot by its very nature sustain its rate of expansion, it is responsible for the boom. The distinction made here is that growth connotes long run continuity and to the degree that our credit methods cannot be forever made more liberal, they are "boom generators." George Shea, when he wrote for the Wall Street Journal, recognized that ". . . . a trend in which debt continues year after year to increase much faster than economic activity, it is obvious that such a trend cannot be sustained indefinitely because the burden of interest on debt and debt-repayment becomes a steadily larger portion of income derived from economic activity."[5] Barron's Financial Weekly stated of the credit expansion as early as 1965 that it "has contributed highly to today's prosperity. By the same token, it has helped create excesses which sooner or later will bring the next deflation."[6]

The very nature of most applications of credit are intrinsically cyclical. Business investment, office and commercial building, home building, stock collateral loans and consumer durable goods constitute primary sponsors for debts, all of which have demonstrated an unquestioned ability to intensify both rises and declines in business activity.

Leon T. Kendall, economist for the United States Savings and Loan League, made a statement in the Commercial and Financial Chronical which could sum up the situation. He said, "Our economy was built on credit and its ready availability."[7] Accompanying the development of this entire superstructure of credit has been the transformation of our attitude toward debt, both individually and collectively.

One young businessman bragged, "I'm in debt for $660 thousand now, and I hope to be in debt for a million and a quarter in three years." This young businessman displayed a common attitude. Even though he was forty years old, his entire adult life had been spent in a period of prosperity. Is it any wonder that he was willing to build a personal financial structure oriented solely to economic expansion?

People who witnessed the last significant economic decline as adults and dealt with its problems are now a minority exerting less and less influence.

In business, the weight that the older generation carries is rapidly declining not only because they are out-numbered, but also because they are reluctant to bear the stigma of impeding progress. The intensifying aggressiveness of business as a result of this declining cautiousness and the growing sense of well-being accelerated. Ever increasing commitments to expand capacity and make investments was the distinguishing characteristic of business in the sixties. Accompanying this has been the use of more and more leverage (borrowed money) to achieve these ambitions.

Government at all levels was under similar influence. If anything, the shorter-run optimistic nature of politics and the completeness of personal success or failure in this field intensified the aggressiveness, recklessness, or abandon, whichever you prefer. The accelerating expansion of state and local government debt offers some testimony to this development. On the federal level, too, the diminishing influence of those who would choose a less aggressive attack on the natural forces of adjustment is obvious. So preponderant was the philosophy of the "New Economics" that those opposing the experiments were quickly singled out for ridicule. This development in government, however, was but an extension of the general attitude of individuals. As personal and family financial structures become more frail, the people who created them went to the polls and elected those who were of the same mind or who offered some promise to enact laws that might prolong the life of their flimsy personal financial structures. The editorialized words of Malcolm M. Forbes back in 1964 struck the tone of the anxieties of that economic path—"Old Ben Franklin might have thought an economist was one who economizes, but today's economists usually preach that if more is spent than taken in, you don't go broke, you go boom. And—for-

24

tunately—they've been right for the last three decades."[8]

The prevailing philosophy of the sixties didn't happen overnight. A study entitled "The New Consumer" made by the Research Division of the Chicago Tribune, as reported, stated, "There has been a shift from the philosophy of security and saving to a philosophy of spending and immediate satisfaction . . . more self-indulgent spending, a tendency to equate standard of living with possession of material goods." "The people of the United States have been thrust into making a more abrupt transformation in their system of values since World War II than in just about any comparable period of time in the nation's history."[9] D. L. Thomas, writing for Barron's noted that ". . . the type of customer seeking loans has changed significantly. Before the war, he was generally a person in financial distress. Today, however, he is an affluent borrower."[10]

The borrower of the sixties was not the person seeking funds for emergencies and necessities, but to secure more luxury. It is a new generation who thinks it prudent to purchase an air-conditioned, luxury automobile on credit when, in fact, they haven't the money to buy a stripped-down, low-priced model for cash. There are others, of the "old school," who would think this appalling. They believe that an automobile without the accessories would be proper under such circumstances. Home buyers depending almost entirely on credit have demanded higher and higher priced homes. As one home builder stated, " . . . home buyers are turning thumbs down on houses unless they offer such features as family rooms, built-in ranges and ovens, carpeting, walk-in closets, and finished basements." There seems to be an even more liberal attitude toward credit as we move down the age scale to our young adults. "Much of the rapid growth in loans is due to early marriages and to more rapid family formation by young adults who demand the good things in life now, without having to save up for them."[11] The older generation has observed with perplexity the acquisition of this great debt by their offspring. In commenting on the problem of college students shunning part-time jobs at school, an official of the University of Minnesota was reported to have declared that "students now tend to borrow more and work less." Student loans have been made easier and more available by the National Defense Education Act (NDEA). Students using the NDEA program, the youngest borrowers of the era, have demonstrated a still less responsible attitude toward debt. A report from a study made by the Office of Education, which administers the program, showed that in the one thousand schools surveyed, $2 million in loans were in default, representing 16.6 per cent of the loans which had become due. By way of comparison, the delinquency rate on installment loans from commercial banks averages about 1.7 percent.

HUMAN JUDGMENT AND YOUR FUTURE

Accompanying these changes in attitude toward debt was a constantly growing optimism. The more time that separates us from unpleasant economic experiences, the faster the aggregate optimism grows. Economists have long recognized that our system is greatly influenced by the businessman's appraisal of the future. If pessimistic, he does not make the capital outlays, and economic activity is slowed. If he is too optimistic, he may well over-invest creating temporary prosperity only to be followed by a recession as the capital stocks become adjusted to need. That is to say, if too many houses, apartments, hotel rooms, restaurants, factories, or too much inventory are built, relative to what the economy can sustain at any one level of income, there will follow a period when few will be built while the adjustments occur. More than at any other time in this country's history, the optimism of the consumer carries great weight among the economic influences. If the consumer is over-optimistic and commits himself excessively to payments greater than he can handle in a period of lesser income, he can set in motion an economic wave.

An officer of a commercial bank expressed the view that one of his most important tasks in life was to protect people from their own optimism. Optimism is a cherished American tradition. Many believe that it has been the most important force in building this great nation. An optimist is always pleasant company. It has always been a failing of man's nature to avoid the unpleasant even at the risk of being uninformed. Quite equally, he is attracted to the pleasant at the risk of being misinformed. Because of the tendency to grab at the pleasant and to shut out the unpleasant, it is no wonder that, at times, optimism reigns unchallenged. While discussing the ostrich-like behavior toward the hazards to our prosperity, an individual commented smugly, "You can't argue with success." True, you can't argue with success—not because your arguments are invalid, but because you won't have any listeners. Man's quest for economic salvation is so strong that he clings to the concepts that are consistent with this aspiration and rejects those which are incompatible regardless of their validity.

Many fortunes have been made by persons who correctly assessed a future economic decline. Many more have been made by those who protected their assets against decline and thereby had the funds to take advantage of depressed prices and find investment opportunities. A more common error of financial judgment has been due to the inability to forecast the good times that have followed the poor times. However, when times are poor, gloom pervades the economy and few continue to have faith in its bright future and unlimited potential.

An example of this is found in the fact that the majority of those dealing in common stock are inept. It is axiomatic that when stock prices are highest, the majority opinion is "bullish" or optimistic, and are lowest when the majority opinion is "bearish" or pessimistic. When considering that success is enjoyed by those who, over the course of the cycle, buy low and sell high, it must follow that the truly successful investors are a minority. When stock prices are rising, all seems well. The higher they rise, the more secure the investor feels—when the opposite should be the case. Stock prices are at their highest when the outlook appears best. Conversely, they are the lowest when gloom reigns supreme and vision is so clouded that the true gems appear as gravel. It is our hope that the following pages will help you join the minority.

In the process of telling the story of money and credit and their influence on the decade of the sixties, a helpful investment analysis develops for lenders and borrowers alike; if a loan turns out badly for the lender as an investment, it is most likely that the borrower too is involved in a most unsuccessful investment. This will be revealed as we discuss such areas as mortgage debt, consumer debt, state and municipal debt, business debt, federal debt and the stock market. It is the element of anticipation or appraisal of the future that is the key to the understanding and acceptance of a fluctuating economy. The level of economic activity is greatly affected by the composite anticipation of all persons operating in the economy and by political events. This anticipation is a human judgment and is, thereby, subject to all of the human errors. As long as man is fallible, there will be economic fluctuations. The greater the influence of any one man's judgment or a small group of men's judgment on the total economy, the more vulnerable to human fallibility will be the economic welfare of the group.

The extensive use of credit permits the error of over-optimism and political instability to have even greater economic consequences. The willingness of the businessmen, the consumer and the politician to use debt has generated a situation that has seemed to justify past commitments to debt as well as further commitments to even more debt. This error of over-optimism also leads to a lowering of the quality of credit extended, the consequences of which are

28

felt more in an economic constriction. If the quality of credit deteriorates enough, as it has for some of our largest cities, what may start out to be the slightest economic decline can develop into one of a greater consequence.

A CREDIT PERSPECTIVE OF THE WHOLE ECONOMY

The whole economy is the sum of its parts. When we examine each major part of our economy from the view of credit and politics, we discover a number of things. We see the effect of many innovations in our credit institutions, and how they have contributed to a long prosperity. We see excesses, abuses and exploitation of the various forms of credit and the way each has exerted a great force toward a rapidly expanding supply of money. We see how the various sectors are interrelated and how expansion or constriction of one sector can provoke a similar response in another. Examination of the economy from this viewpoint illustrates how income circulates through the body of the economy with credit being a primary factor for enabling savings to flow back into that income stream, and how money is the factor which permits it to grow.

This presentation of the economy from a credit viewpoint, it is hoped, will give the reader a perspective of money and credit that will enable him to better appraise the consequences of his government's actions, the trends in the economy, and help him in his own investment and business decisions.

In order to do this, it must be kept in mind that some factors influencing the economy in the various sectors are short-term in nature while others are long-term. Further, some can be working for expansion while others are working for contraction. If the whole economy is the sum of its parts, then the greatest expansion will occur when the parts are all or nearly all expanding simultaneously. The fact that many elements tend to move in the same direction concerns few when that direction is upward. It must be kept in mind that upward forces of many ever present long-term factors such as population growth can be overwhelmed by a downward push by many short-term factors declining simultaneously.

FOOTNOTES

1. Fredrick Duerrenmatt. **The Visit,** an English adaption by Maurice Valency.

2. Simon Kuznets. **Six Lectures on Economics Growth.** The Free Press of Gencoe, Ill., p. 13.

3. **Encyclopedia of Banking and Finance.** Cambridge: Bankers Publishing Company, 1949 p. 76.

4. Alvin H. Hanson. **Business Cycles and National Income.** New York: W. W. Norton, 1951, p. 502.

5. Wall Street Journal, January 25, 1965.

6. Barron's, May 17, 1965.

7. Leon T. Kendall, "Quality of Mortgage Credit." **Commercial and Financial Chronical,** May 14, 1964.

8. Forbes, September 1, 1964.

9. Vance Packard. **The Waste Makers.** David McKay Company, Inc., 1960 p. 233.

10. Barron's, November 30, 1964.

11. Barron's, November 30, 1964.

Chapter III

HOW WE GOT HOOKED

Most of our population does not remember the chaos that followed the stock market crash of 1929 or, for that matter, the financial institutions that existed before it. We tend to take our present institutions for granted and forget the many revelations that occurred since the early 1930's.

It is difficult for many of us to believe that much of the foundation for the boom of the sixties was laid over thirty years before. While the innovations of that time were the product of efforts to deal with the economic collapse, they contributed extensively to the boom. Undoubtedly, few of the people engaged in solving the problems of the troubled thirties could have foreseen the extent to which their innovations would be exploited, for they were concerned with bringing order to the chaotic conditions that existed in our financial community and throughout the economy. These innovators were not designing institutions for the purpose of developing a colossal debt, but rather were concerned with the collapse of the stock market, mortgage market and banking system, as well as the financial trouble of the municipalities, corporations, farmers, savings and loan associations and individuals.

Unemployment had jumped to about one-fourth of the work force. In many or most cases, the families so affected saw their income drop to almost zero. This large portion of our population found that as a result of forces totally beyond their influence, they had been removed from the mainstream of economic activity with only savings and niggardly welfare for sustenance.

Against this backdrop of chaos and deprivation that is almost beyond the comprehension of the subsequent generations who did not witness it, the Congress and the Roosevelt administration having virtually no understanding of the cause tried desperately to enact and implement legislation that could alleviate these conditions. In unprecedented fashion, the Congress enacted remedial legislation that dealt primarily with the symptoms. Like that of most innovators, some of their work was good, some was ineffective, and in this case, some was even unconstitutional.

EARLY HANGOVER REMEDIES

Of the emergency acts passed by the Congress to meet the financial emergencies which followed 1929, the Banking Acts of 1933, 1934, and 1935 did much to strengthen and improve banking. A most important contribution of these acts was the provision for deposit insurance—up to $2,500 initially and amended to $5,000, $10,000 and $15,000 and $20,000 subsequently. This gave depositors new confidence that had been almost completely destroyed by the epidemic of bank failures. It also lessened the risk of "runs" on the banks, and gave the insuring agency the power to influence the bank's investment and reserve policies and to inspect the bank's operations.

Beyond the provisions that strengthened the banks and helped to rebuild confidence in them, the banking acts, like much other work of the Congress, was an effort to liberalize credit for the purpose of providing an inmmediate stimulant to the depressed and seemingly stagnating economy. The Banking Act of 1935 permitted banks to make more liberal real estate loans if secured by a mortgage providing for repayment of at least half of the loan in ten years. Young people today take the amortized [1]—long term mortgage loan for granted. Few realize that prior to 1927, commercial banks could not make urban mortgage loans of more than one year maturity, and from then until the Banking Act of 1935, could not make such loans for more than five years or fifty percent of the property value. As Economist Leon T. Kendall stated it, "We got out of the box by liberalizing the loan contract. We innovated. We switched from the straight loan to the amortized loan. We stretched terms out over a long enough time period so the monthly payments were within the reach of the home buyer." He went on to say, "The great FHA program was built on this premise. Since then the pattern has been one of steady liberalization."[2]

The savings and loan associations, while a relatively small factor, had been making amortized mortgage loans prior to the "crash." Regardless of their small size and amortized loans, they enjoyed no immunity to hard times. The Federal Home Loan Banks were established to strengthen and aid the associations, providing insurance for their shareholder accounts and investment certificates. This was the turning point for these associations, although it took the savings and loans over fifteen years to regain the level of assets that they possessed in 1929. The fantastic rise of the savings and loans to a position of prime importance among our financial institutions occurred in only the most recent years. Thus, the biggest effects of this depression-generated measure did not become evident until about twenty years after the introduction of savings insurance, when the boom was getting underway. James Gillies noted in a study prepared for the Commission on Money and Credit, "Without this insurance, the savings public, mindful of the problems of many commercial instiutions in the 1930's, would probably not have been willing to place their funds in an association—even with the opportunity to earn higher rates of return than in other comparable institutions."[3] The availability of vast amounts of money for home financing and the resulting construction have been among the keystones of our great boom.

Federal credit programs seem to appear in every corner

of our system. The following table from a study prepared for the Commission on Money and Credit covers no less than fifty-one federal domestic lending programs and gives a quick picture of the magnitude of these programs and the areas of greatest quantitative contribution.[4]

(000)	1929	1939	1949	1958
Agricultural Loans	1,947,745	4,779,779	6,080,540	12,244,210
Business Loans	129,073	957,451	1,483,643	1,469,321
Housing Loans	- - -	5,177,521	20,509,087	67,059,777
Miscellaneous Loans	52,130	347,745	179,982	431,546
Total	2,128,948	11,262,493	28,253,252	81,204,854

Many more structural changes were made in the economy in the depression days. The Securities Acts of 1933 and 1934, the Public Utility Holding Company Act, and the Investment Company Act are examples. These were designed to end some specific abuses that had developed in the financial community during the exuberant expansion of the twenties. With the termination of some of these most flagrant abuses of the public interests, the foundation was laid for the re-establishment of public confidence in the securities market. This still took almost twenty years and, as will be discussed in Chapter VII, has turned out to be a very important influence during these "fat years."

Social Security Old Age Benefits and Unemployment Insurance were two programs of major importance that were enacted during the depression. The needs of the elderly did not change suddenly with the depression. The elderly had been neglected for generations, as prior to this time there were few pension and retirement programs. When savings were exhausted, there remained only the alternatives of burdening the children, accepting welfare or being relegated to the old folks' home. Beyond these evident social needs, social security was seen as a means of reducing the work force and, thereby unemployment problems. By establishing an age limit on the work force through this indirect means, the aggregate size of the force could be reduced and the amount of unemployment, in turn, reduced.

Unemployment insurance was seen as a social need during the depression. Persons who were willing to work were unable to do so because of forces completely beyond their control, and their lack of purchasing power as consumers, in turn, caused still others to fall into the same plight. Unemployment insurance was seen as a way of preventing these secondary and snowballing effects of decline. Today's temporarily unemployed still have purchasing power supplied them from the insurance benefits. This slows the cumulative effects of a declining economy and is one of the "built-in stabilizers." The programs of that time initiated the use of federal deficits in time of peace in hopes of bolstering the aggregate demand, and this depression-born concept was employed to force the expansion of the money supply and aggregate demand, heightening the boom. Also products of depression, the socio-economic measures such as social security and unemployment insurance have fostered a lack of concern for the future on the part of the borrowing consumer and this too contributed to the expansion.

These federal programs have had a remarkable influence on the attitudes of the people toward the government's responsibility—not only for what it should do, but what it can do. The federal government has assumed the role of providing a paternalistic refuge. Borrowers and lenders, businessmen and politicians, the young and the elderly, all seem to hold the view that regardless of the difficulty in the economy as a whole, the federal government can and will protect their personal economic security.

A LIBERALIZED ATTITUDE TOWARD
THE STIMULANT

The debt that resulted from the financing of World War II had a profound impact upon the economy and our attitudes both then and subsequently. The unprecedented federal debt which soared from some $50 billion in 1940—which, by the way, was thought very high after a decade of deficits—to roughly $275 billion five years later, was felt in every corner of the economy. Much of this debt was monitized i.e., made part of the money supply. The immediate effects of this were, of course, big pay checks and profits. Because of the abundance of money and the gross lack of consumer goods that resulted from the allocation of production to the war effort, the rationing system was implemented. Without it, the prices of the available goods would have skyrocketed and the inflation would have been immediate rather than shifted to the postwar period. Had the federal government taxed most of this money away directly to pay for the war, the story that followed might have been substantially different. The inflationary forces that were contained by rationing and price controls during the war took hold after the war when the restrictions were removed. Commenting upon the fact that the money stock was multiplied two and one-half times from 1939 to 1945, Friedman and Schwartz wrote, "The money stock grew at a much reduced rate in the early postwar years, yet indexes of prices rose rapidly. That outcome was widely regarded as, at least partly, a delayed reaction to the large wartime increases in the stock of money."[5]

We should mention here that inflation which occurs as a result of financing federal deficits by expanding the money supply is in fact, a hidden tax on savings.[6]

There are certain fundamentals of credit that are oriented around the ability and the willingness of the parties. They are the availability of funds and the willingness to risk them in a loan on the one hand, and the ability and willingness to sustain the debt on the other. These were greatly affected by the war and the war debt. By the beginning of the war, the nation's corporations had been through a terrible decade. For the period from 1929 to 1939, corporate reserves and surpluses were depleted by aggregate losses and dividend payments in excess of earnings, and companies were generally in poor shape to borrow money. The war changed this. Profits rose rapidly, and in spite of a high corporate income tax, undistributed profits were large and financial structures improved. This improved corporate financial condition paved the way for greater corporate debt, which in turn, helped to further improve earnings and financial conditions to allow for still more debt.

Corporate debts have a maturity date but are often refinanced, and therefore, the debt (or leverage) is continued indefinitely. Other debts are amortized or mature and are not refinanced. These loans were continually paid—down through the depression and war. This process also contributed to the potential ability of corporations to incur new debt after the war.

Similarly, local and state governments also were greatly affected by the war. Nearly all state and local bonds are given serial maturities. Commonly, each bond issue matures in part each year until the obiligation is satisfied. This is because the bonds are to be paid, as a rule, from the pledged tax receipts or revenues from a specific capital improvment. During the war years, virtually no resources could be taken from the war effort to build state and local improvements. As a result, the total outstanding state and local debt declined while income—and thus the ability to borrow—increased.[7] This formed a firm foundation upon which to incur debts after the war.

The individual was similarly affected. The opportunity to save during the war was welcomed after a decade of depression. Saving was not only encouraged by war bond drives, but was also in part forced on the consumer by rationing. Big incomes and few services and goods available for which to spend the money left only the alternative of saving. As a result of these new liquid assets, the potential of individuals as borrowers was enhanced considerably. During this period, consumer debt had been reduced to record low levels, but the debt was to be re-established once consumer goods were again plentiful. A decade and a half of declining liquidity and more liberal spending was the springboard from which the nation jumped into the sixties.

POST-WAR DEVELOPMENTS

A number of developments subsequent to World War II are worthy of mention and discussion as contributing factors to the great boom. Some were a direct result of government action, some an indirect result, while others were just a product of the changed technology.

One example of direct government action that liberalized credit in this post-war period was the G. I. loan benefits. Veterans Administration mortgage loan insurance made mortgage loans available to veterans with very small down payments. V. A. insured loans increased from zero in 1944 to $30 billion in 1959.

At the end of World War II, government activity shrank rapidly, but in spite of this, there remained a large fraction of the economy that was dominated by the federal government. Accompanying this development was the philosophy that the federal government bore much responsibility for the level of economic activity. This, after getting a strong start in the thirties and having been reinforced during the war years, manifested itself in the Employment Act of 1946.

Circumstance alone has supplied the reason for much of the government's economic influence since the war. National defense has furnished an almost universally acceptable reason for the government to command directly a sizable fraction of the total economy. Adding to this, the "race for space" supplied a more gratifying area for governmental operations. A more recent, less accepted and more contrived area for governmental influence has been the "War on Poverty."

From the end of World War II through the Eisenhower Administration, there prevailed an attitude that the federal budget should balance. This balance was generally achieved, but in some years slight economic adjustment, or recessions, if you prefer, caused revenues to fail in meeting expectation, or government spending was accelerated and deficits resulted. In 1960, efforts to balance the budget vanished; the new effort was to achieve a deficit, and with this debt, to buy a boom. Until the tight money of 1966, bank lending was virtually forced to become more and more liberal. Two factors were greatly responsible for this. The increasing interest rates paid on savings put the banks under great pressure to promote and seek the highest yielding loans. The ready availability of savings deposits, "on demand," if you please, caused funds to receive high interest in savings accounts that in an earlier time would have remained in checking accounts. Business Week reported as early as 1963, "The sharp increase in time and savings deposits at commercial banks over the past year has aggravated the problem. The press for earnings, to offset higher costs on savings and overhead, is so great that some lenders have gone beyond what they once considered prudent bounds."[8] The high interest rates lured deposits from checking accounts to savings accounts. The rate of growth of demand deposits lagged far behind the growth in level of business activity. In the ten years from 1959 to 1969 for example, demand deposits barely increased one third while savings and time deposits increased some 300%. During much of this period, banks had large excess reserves. The combination of these forces caused the banks to aggressively pursue the borrowers. A midwestern banker was reported to say, "A lender tries to place his money in the best loans available to him. The more money that is around, the lower down the list he goes and the more marginal his loans become."

The fact that the individual banker was at the mercy of these conditions and that the Federal Reserve had control of them, suggests that the intent of the Federal Reserve at the time was to jam money and credit into the economy. The statement, by the then Chairman of the Board of Governors of the Federal Reserve System, "The one factor over which the Federal Reserve has anything like complete control is the volume of reserves available to the banking system,"[9] at least gave an early admission as to where the responsibility really rested.

Another interesting phenomenon of the post-war period was the development of suburbia. The exodus to the suburbs came about as a result of many factors. The automobile, for example, was a major facilitating influence. Indeed, it is difficult to imagine the decentralization without it. While the automobile contributed to the growth of the suburbs, the suburbs have contributed to the growth of the automobile, providing the need and space for two and three cars per family.

But the suburbs have done more to contribute to the prosperity than providing the favorable environment for an automobile boom. The suburbs themselves are extravaganzas dramatizing a multiplicity of debts and credit arrangements. In many instances, the very existence of the suburb is owed to the exploitation of credit. The promoters and developers, operating almost entirely on credit, built houses and trade facilities financed almost entirely on credit.

This, of course, is only the beginning. Think for a moment of the community improvements and requirements that are capital outlays, financed in most cases, largely by credit: schools, sewer systems, water systems, street lighting, hospitals, garbage disposal equipment, fire stations and fire-fighting equipment, and on and on. The expansion of suburbia has necessitated great capital outlays by the public utilities—the phone companies, the power companies and gas companies. These are largely financed by debt.

And that is not the end. The automobile-decentralized

way of life has transformed our commercial life. The central core shopping area became so choked with cars that the outlying shopping centers were a natural outgrowth. The development of drive-in "everythings" was part of this great change. These commercial innovations have been built with borrowed money. They have sprung up everywhere, grand and glorious. It is easy to overlook the fact that these new commercial centers have been "pumping" vast sums of money into the income stream, and many years will pass before they are inadequate or require replacement. Extensive expressways have been built, also on credit, to carry the abundance of automobiles from the suburbs to the cities and back again.

What a wonderful income and debt-generating picture —thousands of commuters driving financed automobiles on bond-indebted expressways past the site of construction of a new shopping center on the way to their mortgaged homes which have financed appliances, boats and camping equipment in the garages. This is a picture unique to this generation.

CONCLUSION

The inhibitions restraining the use of credit had been all but demolished as the nation entered the sixties.

The symptoms of the liquidity crisis of the early 30's were the failure of credit institutions. While the cause of the crisis may well have been obscure, the manifestations of it were not. Massive innovation in the field of credit was undertaken by the federal government to deal with these symptoms. Credit was improved, liberalized, and strengthed. The crisis-born credit innovations subsequently became employed far beyond that which probably was visualized or intended by the innovators. It might well be that this concern for credit and credit institutions that was generated in the depression was the cause of what later developed into an obsession to chase prosperity via the exhaustive exploitation of credit. The other factors of economic expansion seem to be relegated to a backseat, as there developed a fixation upon credit as the most important tool for economic growth.

Also, the financing of World War II appears to have contributed much to the nation's preoccupation with credit. To finance the war, drastic credit measures were employed. The monitization of much of the federal debt which resulted from great deficits in the federal budget, was, indeed, drastic and the consequences were many and far reaching. One consequence was the conditioning of the public to acceptance of an enormous federal debt. This was an important step to the subsequent sanctioning of the expansion of the federal debt for purposes that, when compared to a war for survival, were mere frivolity. Federal deficits were applied in the thirties to "prime the pump." When this "priming" seemed to have failed in 1938, public acceptance of this method remained quite limited. The massive deficits almost universally removed doubts about the potence of federal deficit financing. After fifteen years of learning to live with a large federal debt, federal deficits were euphemistically styled "The New Economics" and the foundation was laid for the ultimate tool of credit exploitation—the credit of the federal government. This extensive use of federal credit provoked an even more intensive application of credit in virtually every sector of the economy. With the rapid expansion of the money supply responding to the excessive demand for credit, saturation became complete. The consequent inflation left no acceptable alternative with which to buy another month, week or even another day of booming prosperity.

FOOTNOTES

1. An amortized loan is one which is made with the provision that principal be repaid along with interest in regular, often equal and monthly payments. This is contrasted by the unamortized loan, which commonly provides for regular interest payments over the life of the loan but with no principal repayment required until the note matures or is due.

2. Kendall, Leon T. "Quality of Mortgage Credit." **Commercial and Financial Chronical,** May 14, 1964.

3. James Gillies. **Federal Credit Programs, Englewood Cliffs, N. J.** Prentice Hall Inc., p. 437.

4. Stewart Johnson. **Federal Credit Programs,** A Study Prepared for the Commission on Money and Credit. Englewood Cliffs, N. J. Prentice Hall Inc.,

5. Milton Friedman and Anna Jacobson Schwartz. **A Monetary History of the United States, 1867-1960;** A study by the National Bureau of Economic Research. Princeton, N. J. Princeton University Press, 1963, p. 13.

6. "In terms of federal government expenditures during the period of wartime deficits, 48 percent was financed by explicit taxes; 7 percent by direct government money creation; 14 percent by private money issue, which can be regarded as the indirect effect of government money creation but had as its nominal counterpart interest-bearing rather than non-interest-bearing government debt; and 31 percent by interest-bearing government securities not matched by money creation. If the wholesale price index is regarded as correctly measuring the price changes during the war, then about one-fifth of the money creation can be regarded as a tax on money balances, four-fifths as voluntary saving embodied in the form of noninterest-bearing monetary assets. This would mean that, in all, slightly over half of expenditures was financed by taxes, and that about one-tenth of the taxes took the form of a tax on money balances. The defects of the price index mean that these figures probably underestimate the importance of taxes as a fraction of expenditures and of the tax on money balances as a fraction of total taxes." Ibid, p. 571.

7. "Statistics on State and Local Government Finance." N. Y., N. Y. **The Bond Buyer,** Vol., 8, 1970, pp. 10, 8.

States, counties, cities, etc., securities outstanding:

    1941 - 19,860,000,000
    1946 - 15,626,000,000

Total state and local revenues (excluding duplicating interlevel transfers)

    1940 - 11,749,000,000
    1946 - 15,983,000,000

8. "Danger Signals Show Up in Credit." **Business Week,** March 16, 1963.

9. William McChesney Martin, Jr. **Supply of Money or Credit,** Federal Reserve Bulletin, August, 1962.

Chapter IV

THE FASCINATING PROPERTIES OF
MONEY AND CREDIT

Like fire, credit can be a valuable servant; and also, like fire, it can burn its user. In the speculative bubbles of history, the use of credit magnified the successes but it also accelerated the failures. The glorious benefits derived from the leverage which credit provides are almost irresistible lures. It possesses the ability to generate the illusion of something for nothing. Because excessive use of credit seems at the time to be sound, individuals, businesses, and nations have fallen prey to this financial Lorelei. How could anything so delightfully beneficial possibly be imprudent?

Credit performs some quite curious functions in our system, some of which are unique to the recent expansion. Certainly, innovations of credit have been profuse in this period and might even be said to characterize the era. An understanding of some of the relationships of these devices to the operations of the economy is essential to the appreciation of their significance. It is to some of these functions that the remainder of this chapter is addressed.

Credit is absolutely essential to the operation of our highly developed and highly specialized economy. Currency and check money (demand deposits) are very essential credit instruments. As a matter of fact, while currency and coin amounted to some $40 billion by the late sixties, checking accounts amounted to about $150 billion. It should be noted that check money overshadows currency by nearly four to one. Money is distinguishable from other types of credit instruments. Much of the power of money as an economic influence is still not well understood. It has been discerned

47

that changes in the quantity of this peculiar type of instrument correlate highly with changes in economic activity.

In recent years, we have learned to operate as consumers with little cash and a wallet full of credit cards. Today you can travel and shop without a dime in your pocket. The magical words "charge it" or "here is my credit card" can substitute for currency almost everywhere. It is hard to imagine what amounts of currency would be required if there were no charge accounts or credit cards.

Installment credit has been the enabling factor which allows much of the population to obtain expensive consumer durables. George Shea, writing for the Wall Street Journal, noted, "Young married couples in many cases couldn't begin to own the washing machines and other labor-saving devices needed in today's homes if it were not for the consumer credit system that this nation has been foremost in developing." He went on to say, "The auto industry would not be as big or prosperous as it is without consumer credit."[1]

Human nature is such that saving before the purchase is difficult while through the use of installment credit, saving after the purchase is enforced by the continuing threat of losing its convenience. Even the Russians have this illogical infirmity and have had to make installment credit available. Installment credit provides broad markets for these expensive durables—markets that are essential for their mass production and the resulting efficiencies and high productivity. The employment of amortized loans to permit individuals to purchase homes has been exploited to an unprecedented degree. The relatively large sums required for the purchase of a home would be prohibitive to a large majority of our families without this credit. By merely rearranging the financial structure that provides capital for investment in housing, the individual can be the landlord and can assume responsibility for the liabilities of ownership. This was accomplished by extending the duration of the amortized loan and requiring smaller down payments, and has been assisted in many cases by supplying federal insurance guaranteeing payment of the loan.

This innovation in credit has been a more subtle effect on our total housing picture. There is a fundamental difference in attitude toward a rented residence as compared to an owned residence. Regardless of the fact that the occupant of a home has only a small amount invested, the feeling that he "owns the house" commonly influences him to be a far more careful resident than if he is "just renting" someone else's house. The care and concern for the preservation and improvement of a structure by the owner-resident is rarely experienced in rental housing. This pattern so basic in human nature gives great validity to this capitalistic method of home ownership. It would seem beyond the most venturesome imagination to conceive the socialist system of government-owned housing as ever enjoying the tender, loving care given most of our privately owned residences.

Essential to the capital formation of our great industrial and commercial complex has been the use of a wide variety of credit instruments. Large quantities of long-term funds have been provided through the employment of these instruments to build the railroads, the utilities, the factories, the stores and virtually every great business enterprise. Widely varying short-term business capital needs—primarily inventory—historically have been supplied by the banking system.

The very nature of public capital improvements such as sewers, streets, and schools require funded debt. The outlays are so much greater than the annual revenue available for them that payment over some portion of the "life" of the improvement is essential. Credit is indeed essential and beneficial to our economy.

Beyond these obvious functions of trade and commerce, credit performs some other more subtle but extremely valuable economic functions—functions without which this prolonged prosperity undoubtedly would not have occurred. Credit instruments are the most important vehicle used to place savings back into the income stream, but ownership securities in the form of newly issued common stock and elements of ownership equities in housing and business also preform this function.

It has long been observed by economists that the savings process tends to take funds from the economy—from the income stream.[2] The investment process returns these funds to the income stream. It must be kept in mind that while these are quite separate functions, and that with the help of intermediaries—banks and other financial institutions— the two tend to remain quite equal. This is to say that savings do find their way back into the income stream rather readily. On the other hand, investment can exceed current savings through the expansion of the supply of money and thereby promote expansion.[3]

People often jest about a "money tree." As astonishing as it might be to many, our system, figuratively speaking, has a money tree. This money yielder is, of course, the commercial banking system. An understanding of this power and the basic ramifications of it is essential to the appreciation of the factors that have influenced and will continue to influence our economic wellbeing. It is important to understand that banks making loans create money and that repayment of bank loans extinguishes money. An excellent explanation of this is given by Abba P. Lerner:

"*Whenever there is an increase in* the total amount of cash in the country, a certain proportion of it finds its way into the coffers of the banks. If the banks keep a reserve ratio of one-tenth (that is, if they keep their cash reserve at about one-tenth of their total deposits), it follows inescapably that for every additional cash dollar obtained by the banks they create ten dollars of bank money or deposits. The power of the banks to create money has frequently been condemned by re-

formers as a usurpation of the money-creating preroga-
tives of the state, but until the 1920s the possession of
this power was commonly denied by bankers.

The banker would deny that anyone bringing an additional $1,000 of cash into his bank would enable him
to increase his deposits by anything like the $10,000
that the theory called for. He would plead that he could
increase deposits only by the $1,000 entered into the
account of the individual who brought in the cash
money. He could perhaps lend out the $900 of spare
cash that would be available after putting aside $100
out of the $1,000 as the 10% reserve against the
new $1,000 deposit, and such a loan of $900 would
mean the creation of $100 of additional bank money.
But the $900 of newly created bank money would dis-
appear as soon as the borrower made use of the $900 he
had borrowed, so that very soon the new credits would
be back at $1,000 rather than $10,000.

This apparent discrepancy arises because the theory
refers to the whole banking system and not to any individual banker. When we look at the whole banking
system we find that the creation of bank money does
not come to an end with the $1,000 created by the first
bank. This is because the first bank, lending the $900
of cash, keeps only one-tenth of the additional cash.
The remaining cash can go from bank to bank, leaving
one-tenth of its amount each time at every bank where
it sojourns, so that when the whole $1,000 cash has
been absorbed, the total amount of additional bank
money created by all the banks together amounts to
$10,000. As long as the sum of new loans, and so of the
new deposits, amounts to less than $10,000, the addi-
tional cash needed for additional reserves is less than
$1,000 and there is still some spare cash permitting
some banks to make still more loans. The sum of new
loans and of deposits therefore keeps on increasing.

51

Only when they amount to $10,000 is the additional $1,000 of cash money entirely absorbed as additional cash reserves at the same ratio of 10%."[4]

MONEY VERSUS CREDIT

Money consists of credit instruments that possess certain characteristics that in combination distinguish them from other credit instruments. These characteristics include the functions of serving as a medium of exchange, a measure of values, a unit of account, a standard of deferred payments, and a store of value. For this reason, we speak of money and credit as separate entities. While the distinctions are not always clear-cut, we have come to define money as currency plus deposits in commercial banks with only small adjustments.

Money works in quite a different way from credit, and has some peculiar characteristics. People frequently believe that the cost of money is measured in terms of interest rates. Interest rates measure the costs of credit, not money. The cost for accumulating money is measured in terms of forebearance of consumption. If the nation demands larger cash balances, it obtains these larger cash balances by foregoing consumption and investment expenditures. This is quite a different cost from the interest rates, and contributes substantially to money's distinction from credit.

Bank lending and investing can expand the quantity of money and the repayment of these can demolish money. Also federal borrowing from the banking system can expand the stock of money. As a result, the quantity of money much of the time in the past has been a product of economic and political forces. An impertant point to remember is, however, that the Board of Governors of the Federal Reserve System, commonly called the "Fed," has the power and authority to determine the quantity of money, the political and economic forces notwithstanding.

It must be borne in mind that there is a distinction between what the Fed did and what it could have or might have done. As we look to the future we will conjecture what the Board might or should do with respect to the quantity of money. In the past, political and economic forces have been dominant factors in effecting changes in the stock of money.

Much of the economic story of the sixties is told here in terms of forces that have influenced money and the economy. The major distortions in the growth rate of money and the attendant inflation or recession occurred with the Fed being an abettor if not the prime determiner.

Income is affected not only by changes in the quantity of money circulating in the income stream, but also by the velocity or speed at which it circulates, i.e. the frequency with which it changes hands. A decreasing rate of turnover is symptomatic of a conservative trend, while a rising velocity indicates a spendthrift trend. Since World War II and through the sixties we have experienced an ever rising rate of turnover of money.

The relationship between expanding income and the instruments of credit are at times intriguing. The creation of money, as we have suggested, tends to cause an increase in total dollar income. It is the income that supports loans.

In the case of the consumer, his income has become extensively allocated to debt service of his home mortgage, automobiles, appliances and furniture payments. Commonly, a pay-raise is committed to payments on still other durables such as a dishwasher, television or perhaps, a boat.

In effect, the consumer has tended to "capitalize" his additional income in debt. Because of the incongruity of the words "capitalize" and "debt", a new word may be coined to describe this process—"debtize." Some consumers have become more skilled in *debtizing* than others. The variables involved are the length of the period for repayment, if the loan and the interest rate are amortized. These can vary greatly depending on the type of loan. Some have managed to sustain much greater debt than others with the

53

same amount of income. So often today, the most skilled in the art of *debtizing* enjoy the highest standard of living or in the popular jargon, the "good things of life."

State and local governments practice *debtizing*. The Boards and Commissions seldom allow much time to elapse between the development of a new source of revenue and its commitment to a new bond issue. Community needs have indeed been pressing, but regardless of the need, it is hard to imagine the legislature or commission that would have funds available for which it had no "absolutely essential" pet project.

It should be apparent from this discussion that the level of disposable income is vital to our gigantic debt structure. Consumers have at times debtized at a rate faster than their disposable income has expanded and as a result their debt burdens have become ever greater. For many, any significant decline in disposable income would be absolutely overwhelming. For others, the fright of such a situation would provoke saving if only by their making an effort to reduce existing debts and gain greater liquidity. The consequences of such an event would serve to restrict incomes still further. The magic of the expansionist is achieved by wielding a two-edged sword which threatens, at the first misjudgment, to lop off his own head.

It becomes apparent that essential to sound economic growth is stability in the rate of growth of the money stock permitting stability in the relationship of income to debt or debt service. If debt service were to grow faster than income, trouble could well be in the offing. If incomes decline, debt service rarely declines gracefully and this spells trouble. Prices, interest rates and taxes affect debt service costs and the income available for debt service. Instability in these relationships can also weaken the economic structure.

We have tried in a confined manner to show the role of money and credit in the expansion of incomes and hence the economy. A rapidly expanding supply of money will tend to cause the economy to expand to its physical limits.

54

Beyond this, inflation will result. In addition to inflation, such an event fosters manifold maladjustments such as labor unrest, speculative stock markets, too rapid accumulation of capital goods, inordinantly high interest rates, speculative building construction and foreign trade imbalances to name a few. A constriction in the quantity of money will tend to cause a constriction in incomes, which, because of the structure of the economy, can terminate economic expansion. Money and credit possess great leverage in their influence on the economy. Small changes in these can generate massive changes in the economy as a whole. The use of such leverage toward expansion inspires little concern and is thereby subject to abuse. The fact is, however, that because of the immense leverage that money and credit have on the entire economy, if we are to seek stability in economic growth, we are obligated to achieve reasonable stability in the growth rate of money.

FOOTNOTES

1. George Shea. **Wall Street Journal,** January 25, 1965.

2. For our purposes, saving is any act which in and of itself withdraws or withholds funds from the income stream. This includes the retention of currency; the placing of funds with an institution which without the additional act of investing, the funds do not flow back into the income stream, or the liquidation of any part of any outstanding debts.

3. For our purposes money consists of currency, demand deposits (checking accounts) and time deposits (savings account and certificates of deposits).

4. Reprint by permission, © Encyclopaedia Britannica, 1946.

Chapter V

HALLUCINATIONS

Have consumers "gone off the deep end" in their use of credit? Have they been tricked by the giant corporate villains into overburdening themselves with debt? Has hypnotic advertising made them buy things they didn't want?

At no other time or place in the history of the world has the consumer had it so good. His options now are unequalled. Essential to freedom is the opportunity for alternatives —to be able to choose among many products, styles, colors, makes, and prices. Compared to socialist countries or for that matter to any earlier point in time, people as consumers have never had so much freedom. Contrary to what some would have us believe, this unparalleled freedom has been made possible by the great corporate structure of the capitalistic system and the specialization and technology that make individuals so enormously productive. While the system and credit gave the consumer freedom, the government generated a climate which led many consumers to misuse and misjudge the use of their credit. Freedom contains implicitly the freedom to make mistakes, for without that potential there is no freedom. This does not excuse the government for generating unsustainable boom, distorting perspectives and making it virtually impossible for the average family to make correct judgments about its future income, future cost of living, or future value of its assets.

If government has any business at all, it should be to provide economic stability. It has, instead, forced the consumer to struggle through a fantastic obstacle course of economic instability caused by monetary mismanagement and abuse.

This has run from the great depression to the inflationary boom of the sixties.

CONSUMER CREDIT

Everywhere people are observed manipulating credit to improve or sustain their standard of living. Hillel Black pointed out at the beginning of the decade in question that "100,000,000 Americans buy now, pay later."[1] During the ten years that followed, the proliferation of credit cards has been incredible. One estimate is that some 60,000,000 people now carry bank credit cards such as Master Charge and Bankamericard. While the early push in bank credit cards dates back to the early fifties, the great growth occurred in the sixties.

We all know people who seem to constantly walk the tightrope of credit, juggling payments to placate their creditors. Some have referred to this as budgetary brinkmanship. All of us are consumers having this one universal area of common interest, therefore it is little wonder so much conversation is allocated to consumer credit. Consumerism is not unworthy of this attention although at times too much stress is given it at the expense of even more crucial issues.

The following table shows the rapid growth of consumer installment debt.

CONSUMER INSTALLMENT CREDIT[2]

	Auto Paper	Other Consumer Goods	Home Improve-ment	Personal	Total
1960	17.7	11.5	3.1	10.5	42.8
1965	28.6	18.6	3.7	20.4	71.3
1969	36.6	27.6	4.0	29.9	98.1

58

The importance of consumer credit to the "growth" of the economy caused the development of a new school of economic thinking, which might be called the "Consume and Boom" school.

Fluctuations in the demand for durable goods may have a great impact on the level of economic activity. The large amount of credit employed in their procurement combined with the ability to delay replacement can initiate significant moves in the level of business in either direction. Moves upward go unquestioned, but moves downward provoke great re-examination of our institutions. The move by the consumer toward economizing in automobile transportation in 1957 and 1958 was a good example of the importance of the factor which motivated great agonizing over the merits of high horsepower, "superfluous chrome," and "gaudy tail fins." The experience of the auto industry during those years was a harbinger of the economic adjustment of 1970 which showed that the consumer can, indeed, change his patterns and, what is more, that the change can have far-reaching effects on the economy as a whole. The continuous evolution of the attitude of the consumer toward debt contributed much to the boom. But we know from experience that conditions can arise which greatly modify the speed and direction in which consumers are moving with respect to debt. The rate of accumulation of consumer durable goods and the rate of investment in housing can change drastically and this can have a marked effect on investment by business in capital goods.

When dealing with consumer credit, we must include all debts that are the consumer's obligation and which are paid directly from the consumer's disposable income. Most mortgage debt, while it is a type of investment, rests on the consumer. Often, individuals incur mortgage debts, the proceeds of which are spent for purposes other than housing. Similarly, security collateral loans (loans made against the pledge of stock or bonds) are commonly made to supply the consumer with funds apart from the acquisition of additional securities. Notwithstanding the fact that many of these loans can be self-liquidating, the burden of liquidation and interest rests, for the most part, directly on the individual. This type of loan is treated to a larger extent later.

CONSUMER ATTITUDE TOWARD DEBT

The attitude of the consumer toward debt has changed noticeably since the depression and war years. During the depression of the tnirties, many follies of the 1920's came home to roost. Debt became the villain which robbed the consumer of his investments, his home, his furniture, and considerable sleep. The financial chaos of the thirties begot a reluctantly wiser generation. The war years gave people an opportunity to get back on their financial feet. The patriotic war bond drives, the chance to save, and the dearth of goods to buy, fostered the attitude of living for tomorrow—living for the time when the boys would come home. This is a far cry from the "I deserve to have it now on credit" attitude so prevalent in the last decade.

A major contributor to the transformation of public attitude toward debt has been the longevity of the boom. Most came to believe that what they were experiencing was jusc a normal progression—a "natural growth"—and found it difficult to imagine any other way. Armed with this confidence, one finds that the acquisition of large debt seems not only sound, but even wise.

The role of government assisted the development of that new attitude toward debt. It became far from uncommon to hear in rebuttal to a remark about the possible hazards to the economy, "They (meaning the federal government) won't let it decline." This not uncommon attitude implicitly assumed that the federal government had the ability to surmount whatever circumstances might arise, and furthermore, that it would use this ability at the right time and place, and in the proper degree. Unmistakably, the Congress is committed to doing whatever it can to promote and protect prosperity. But what is there to insure the infallibility of the Congress when making decisions in this pursuit?

Confidence has been developed over the years in such programs as Federal Deposit Insurance, Federal Home Mortgage Insurance, Federal regulation of securities markets, Federal Farm Administration, Unemployment Insurance and Social Security. No thought is given to the fact that the effectiveness of these institutions during a major economic decline is still unknown. Even if this sense of security in federal paternalism is not sound, it is comforting. D. L. Thomas pointed out, "Relying on Social Security, private pensions and group life and health insurance plans to take care of a rainy day, Americans are going into debt to buy material comforts."[3]

With an abundance of credit available to all, this natural inclination has been intensified. This has encouraged families to emulate others with means far greater than their own. An outgrowth of this has been a general delusion about wealth. The delusion is perpetrated on others and then, upon the perpetrator himself. A family with little net worth will buy a luxury automobile and an impressive home. Friends and neighbors unaware of their poor balance sheet give them the benefit of the doubt and believe them to have commensurate wealth. Quite often the deception is perpetrated on one another. Vance Packard addressed this with, "American families in the past few years have been giving more and more thought to the problem of establishing a home that adequately reinforces the status image they wish to project of themselves." He further pointed out that, "A speaker at the 1958 convention of home builders in Chicago was reported to say 'home buyers are buying themselves a symbol of success' . . ."[4]

The extensive use of credit makes it virtually impossible to judge a person's wealth from observing his home and other possessions. Many of the apparent wealthy have a negative net worth. If the deception were to be practiced

61

only on others it wouldn't be so bad, but the worst is that it is practiced on themselves. "By striving to buy the product —say, wall to wall carpeting on installment—the consumer is made to feel he is upgrading himself socially."[5] Next we observe that the consumer begins to believe he has thus bettered himself and starts measuring his achievements in terms of acquired possessions. People will reflect and say to themselves, "I now possess a new car, a new home, new furniture, and a new boat. What an accomplishment in these few years!" A rapidly accelerating race has developed among consumers to stay abreast or ahead of their friends in order to appease their egos. No consideration is given to the balance sheet and actual net worth, so he does not share credit for his accomplishments with the larger contributor —debt financing. The delusion has succeeded.

Credit is a wonderful tool which the consumer can use to improve his condition. Like many tools, if mishandled it can be quite hazardous. By design, or in the "school of hard knocks," we learn its dangers. While the lessons learned at the school of hard knocks are indelible, the tuition is often quite high.

ADDITIONAL FACTORS

Debt is often incurred by individuals when there seems to be little need for it. People with sufficient cash and savings will borrow to purchase durables, and even a home. Quite commonly, families will take a maximum mortgage on their new home when they could, in fact, make a substantially larger down payment and bear a proportionately smaller debt. James S. Duesenberry remarked: "Many families . . . do take installment credit while still holding liquid assets. They do so, in part, because they have greater flexibility of action . . . In addition, some families feel that they are sure to pay for installment debt, whereas they fear that once they part with their (liquid) assets they will never be able to save to get them back . . . families with liquid assets feel that they are taking less risk in taking on installment than those with non-liquid assets."[6] If, for those people, income becomes insufficient to meet the monthly obligation, it may be expected that these liquid assets will be used to meet the monthly payments. Thus, liquid assets provide the economy with a buffer against short periods of decline. Longer periods of reduced income will result, for many families, in the liquid assets being used up. While the using-up of these liquid assets mitigates the economic decline, their reestablishment retards the economic recovery.

The greater use of credit enlarged the impact upon the economy of changes in the consumers' preference for liquidity. As consumers face uncertainty, they prefer greater liquidity—which requires a greater rate of saving, less borrowing, and implicitly lower consumption. The exploitation of every facet of economic expansion and consumer optimism during the sixties set the stage for an adjustment and retrenchment of consumer aggressiveness.

Ancillary to the consumer credit explosion has been a booming life insurance business. Consumers, while refusing to make any overt admissions of their precarious personal economic structure, have instinctively purchased unprecedented quantities of life insurance. The consumer, aware that all his achievements—his possessions—are his only as long as his salary is available to make the payments, worries about the worthlessness of his estate. The answer, of course, is life insurance—one more periodic payment to insure that his family can keep these mortgaged possessions if he should die. Income has become so *debtized* that the threat of sickness of the breadwinner is an appalling contemplation. Even a partial loss of income would result in repossession of the family's "assets" and gigantic lowering of the standard of living for many millions of American families. Households so managed are great prospects for the insurance salesman promoting "income protection" insurance in case of disability. One of the greatest single vendors of these life insured and income protection policies is the rapidly expanding consumer debt burden.

One element of consumerism that has been a favorite whipping boy of the consumer advocates is the "planned obsolesence" generated by automobile styling. They have completely missed the point that this "style obsolesence" has been a major factor in the redistribution of the wealth in a manner quite suited to their prejudice—it takes from the rich and gives to the poor. What they may not like is that the rich participate quite voluntarily and much of the time quite eagerly. The mechanics are simple. Because of style consciousness, the market value of automobiles declines much more rapidly than the actual depreciation or wear of the machine. Thus, a $5,000 car after a few years may be only fractionally "used-up," say one-fifth, yet this well-cared-for vehicle may have depreciated four-fifths in sale value. Who benefits? The poor benefit! By virtue of this system a poor person can acquire a car with an intrinsic value of two or three thousand dollars for a few hundred dollars. If style obsolesence didn't exist in this country, far fewer of our less productive and less fortunate citizens would own automobiles at all. Many others would drive vehicles having much less real value and far fewer families would enjoy two or more cars. We need only observe Russia or the underdeveloped countries where the market for used cars remains high. In such places, often only the well-to-do get to drive even used cars. Much of the time this elite minority is delighted to drive cars that would make most Americans feel deprived.

CONCLUSION

The policies of the federal government during the sixties of thwarting even the slightest economic adjustment aided the tendency of the consumer to take on more debt. Recklessness on the part of borrowers and a substantial lack of caution on the part of lenders was fostered by the length

64

of the expansion and the magnitude of the boom. Many people lost concern for or forgot the personal financial problems that economic instability can bring. Many others never knew them.

Manifestly, some of the excesses of consumer credit became a factor in the recession which President Nixon inherited. Whatever excesses developed, however, are more appropriately attributed to poor government and the poor money management of the sixties, rather than to any inherent inadequacies of borrowers and lenders. Give the lenders and the borrowers a more stable economy in which to operate, avoiding the government-generated boom and the recession that must follow, and they will generally act to protect their own best interest—their judgments and perspectives not being distorted by the governmental perversion of economic events.

FOOTNOTES

1. Hillel Black. **Buy Now, Pay Later,** New York. William Morrow & Co., 1961, p. 16.

2. From the Federal Reserve Bulletins

3. D. L. Thomas, "The Personal Touch." Barron's, Nov. 30, 1964.

4. Packard, **The Status Seekers** pg, 54.

5. Ibid, P. 272.

6. James S. Duesenberry, **Business Cycles and Economics Growth.** New York, N.Y.: McGraw-Hill Book Co. Inc., 1958.

Chapter VI

REAL STIMULATION

Real estate mortgages constitute one of the most important categories of debt. It is important not only because of
its sheer size, but its explosive exploitation during the sixties made it a major contributor to the prosperity. In a study
by the National Bureau of Economic Research, it is pointed
out that by 1953, "Urban mortgages had become one of the
most important components of the nation's credit structure,
exceeding in size the net long term debt of the entire corporate sector of the economy."[1]

When one realizes that in the years from 1960 to 1969,
this type of debt has doubled from 206.8 billion to 425.3
billion,[2] it is easier to appreciate how much our prosperity
has been influenced by it. The *annual* increase in the 1960's
was almost equal to the entire real estate mortgage debt
outstanding prior to 1945. The amount of mortgage debt
outstanding by the middle sixties exceeded the total federal
debt.

Physical evidences of this credit are apparent everywhere.
The sprawling suburbs, the profusion of shopping centers,
the multitude of eating establishments, the plethora of small
industrial building, and, in more recent years, the skyline
of high-rise apartment and office buildings have transformed every metropolis in the nation. Many cities, whose sky-
lines had remained unaltered for three decades, changed
greatly in the 1960's.

The mortgage debt is commonly divided into major categories. "One to four family" dwellings support about two-
thirds of it, and the burden of carrying this debt rests essentially on individuals. About one-third of the debt is

backed by multi-family dwellings and commercial properties which are primarily corporate responsibilities.

Expanding business and optimism encouraged small businessmen to build new and modern facilities. The mathematics of debt service and the availability of mortgage money help facilitate these improvements, while larger profits make it possible for businesses to pay higher rents and create an atmosphere in which businesses are more inclined to select spacious offices. The rationalizations of the self-indulgent businessman are more effective when profit margins are high. For many, the pride of operating an attractive, prosperous looking establishment is a sufficient impetus. Office buildings have sprung up all over, from the attractive single unit doctors office to high skyline-changers. All sorts of new debt-laden commercial structures have appeared in recent years as a result of these factors.

To gain more insight into this situation we note James S. Duesenberry's suggestion that the demand for store and office space is governed by the "aggregate real income" and rents. According to Duesenberry, "there is a rapid turnover of firms in most of the trade and service fields, . . . and we can therefore suppose that the amount of (store and office) space occupied depends on the number of firms which can survive under existing conditions."[3] The number of firms that can survive under conditions of booming expansion is considerably greater than in a period of stability or contraction. Because the general economic expansion has dominated the last decade, many gross errors of business judgment have been covered up by the resiliency of the expanding economy.

As the "disposable income" has increased, many service industries have grown to prominence that were relatively insignificant before the days of widespread prosperity. The expanding disposable income has had remarkable effects on such businesses as restaurants, boat distributors, travel agencies and the like. Greater income makes more money available for the luxury trades. Large sums of mortgage money have been allocated to the housing of these rapidly growing businesses.

SOME FACTORS AFFECTING RESIDENTIAL CONSTRUCTION

We are living more and more luxuriously and few care to question how or why. The National Association of Home Builders reported that in 1963 the average new home contained 1206 square feet and in 1964, 1254 square feet, and an average of 1300 square feet in 1965.

One reason for this is that more/than half of the families that bought new homes in the two decades preceding the 1960's had theretofore been renters. It is estimated that in the sixties two-thirds of all new house buyers already were home owners making payments and trading up to improve their situation. One builder was reported to have said, "We're simply not going to entice a family out of the house they're now in by offering them warmed over models at higher prices. What we've got to do is offer them more house. The job is to sow the seeds of discontent with what they now have." Such efforts have apparently succeeded. The average stay in a home has continued to shorten., Although influenced greatly by the mobility of our population for employment reasons, many move to a new home as a "move up" to a larger and more luxurious house. Such statistics as an average stay of five or perhaps seven years in a home are seemingly incongruous with the twenty- and thirty-year mortgages arranged for such transient residents.

The trend is demonstrated by the Housing Acts passed by Congress. The 1964 Housing Act, for example, lowered the down payment requirement for FHA insured loans on single family dwellings from 25% of the amount over $20,000 to 20%. In an earlier time, it might have seemed ostentatious and imprudent for a family with only four or five thousand dollars, to live in a $30,000 home. But the trend has been to live at the outer limits of one's income. The day is virtually gone when the nature of a man's home reflects his wealth. Today, at best, it reflects nothing more than his income— and at that only his income at the time.

The impact of residential construction on incomes in all sectors of the economy and, in turn, the impact of expanded incomes on the rate of residential construction, present an intriguing cycle. Mortgage money supplied for housing by the banking system, saving & loans, insurance companies and others finds its way quite directly into the hands of tradesmen, building suppliers, realtors, financing arrangers, attorneys, and building contractors. More indirectly, it finds its way to steel workers, aluminum workers, lumber industry workers, tool manufacturing workers and so on. These people then spend it for cars, food, clothing and all manner of services and thus the monies filter throughout economy. Again the added income stimulates more residential construction as it becomes *debtized* (pledged to the service of more debt) and still more mortgage money flows into the economy. As Professor Duesenberry stated ". . . the rate of investment in housing influences the rate of growth of aggregate income, which in turn influences the demand for housing."[4] He observed that in the 1920's the rate of building reached a very high level partly because it helped to increase the rate of growth of aggregate income.[5] Clearly we have exploited this cumulative effect of building construction by employing a remarkable number of innovations in credit and thereby directing savings away from other investments.

This type of expansion will undoubtedly remain with us until the exploitation of credit produces excesses either in the total supply of housing or in certain categories of housing.

REDUCTION IN QUALITY OF MORTGAGE CREDIT

In practice, the conventional safeguards of lending have been twisted, stretched, and side-stepped for pleasure and profit. Limitations as to the terms of the loan, the ratio of the value of the real estate to the amount of the loan, and the ability of the borrower to repay the loan are generally imposed limitations designed to protect both the lender and the borrower. The lenders—usually institutions—often found during the sixties that such rules seemed at times to hinder their ability to make profits and the borrowers—often consumers—found that the rules prevented them from living in the way to which they imagined they were entitled. With both parties to the loan agreement desirous of bending the rules to permit the loan, it is no wonder that the bending occurred.

Dr. Saul B. Klaman, Director of Research of the National Association of Mutual Savings Banks, addressing this problem, said, "Another basic result of the mortage scramble—though not statistically measurable—has been a reduction in the quality of credit. By this I mean the willingness of lenders to qualify marginal borrowers not earlier acceptable, wink at overly liberal property appraisals, extend contract maturities, and reduce down-payment requirements."[6]

The continued easing of credit terms was one of the most outstanding characteristics of that boom. It takes only minor lulls in the level of residential real estate activity, however, to cause lenders to mend their ways. Transgressions from the rule of sound mortgage investing quickly become apparent even in short, mild, slowdowns in housing as poor loans go bad.

Although fraud is seldom thought of as being widespread enough to be of any major consequence, it was so commonly employed in some areas to produce real estate mortgage loans that few thought of it as dishonest. One home owner tells of his experience: "When my wife and I were looking for a home, we found one about 35 years old that we liked very much. The advertised price was $19,500. On homes of this vintage, the loan limit was 60% and this would have required $7,800 down payment. When we told the realtor that we had only $5,000, he informed us that in such cases two

71

agreements are executed—one for the record and for the benefit of the lending institution, in this case an insurance company, and one for the buyer and seller. A "purchase price" of $25,000 was suggested for the transaction so that the loan would be $15,000 and we would then need only $4,500." He went on to say, "We were appalled at the nonchalant manner in which this fraud was proposed; we started to inquire around. An attorney told us, 'Well, that's just the way it's done.' A builder we questioned about the practice suggested, 'That is the only way I can stay in business.' "

More frequently, this type of manipulation was done for buyers of newly constructed houses. The loan limits on this housing have commonly reached 80% or 90% of the appraised value or the amount of the sale price, whichever is lower. For example, the builder and purchaser agree on a price of $18,000 for a house. The down payment would normally be $1,800 on a 90% loan. To circumvent this down payment, the buyer and builder fake a contract that shows a sale price of $19,500. The appraiser approves the $19,500 price and the 90% or $17,550 loan is granted, so that now the buyer need only raise $450 for the down payment.

The Wall Street Journal reported, "Through conspiracies involving various combinations of builders, real estate and mortgage brokers, lawyers, appraisers, and sometimes loan company officials themselves, borrowers are finding it possible to sometimes obtain a house or property with little or no cash investment of their part." "The trend," the article went on to say, "has become so worrisome that federal and state authorities are launching investigations of the practice; the Justice Department, for example, currently is looking into allegations of fraud in home mortgages in such cities as New York, Chicago, and Los Angeles." Further it reported, "The fraud is sometimes so wide-spread that it involves entire housing subdivisions."[7]

Under conditions of high employment and rising property values, this practice appears to be a virtue rather than a vice; more beneficial than the thefts of Robin Hood. Everyone seemed to benefit—the borrower, the brokers, the builders, the attorneys—and even in some cases, the lenders. These frauds seem not only morally right, but almost patriotic as they assisted our "Gross National Product" to grow. The wrong done by these acts of deceit may appear later in the mortgage defaults and foreclosure statistics, but that true test would come only under trying economic conditions.

The low down payment mortgage loan, whether obtained through FHA, VA, or some other means, is the most vulnerable to deterioration of economic conditions. Buyers can obtain housing this way often for less than rent and have little or nothing to lose if it becomes expedient to abandon the house.

Rising delinquencies during that period of unparalleled prosperity suggest that there are some basic inadequacies in the methods. Certainly, improvement in general economic conditions could not be looked to for a correction of that situation and when the economic conditions weaken, the rate of delinquency could be expected only to worsen.

Another innovation on the credit scene is the real estate mortgage loan for purposes other than the acquisition or improvement of the property. To preceding generations, the height of impropriety was to mortgage the home for any reason other than absolute essentials. By contrast, the sixties ushered in a new era. During long periods in which mortgage money was overflowing, mortgage loans were obtained for all manner of non-real-estate purposes, and often for outright frivolity. The loans were made to prepay other shorter-term loans to reduce debt service. They frequently were made to cover the cost of college for the children. Also, real estate mortgage loans for furniture, pleasure boats, cars, planes, and travel abroad were reported.

One practice that developed during a period of plentiful mortgage money was the extension of an existing mortgage loan, sometimes called by one savings and loan association a "Zipper Loan." The mortgager, having brought his mortgage down over the years, could return to the lending insti-

73

tutions and extend the term of the mortgage back to the original length or longer, receive the additional cash and have the same payments to which he was accustomed. Also, borrowers have been going to other institutions and refinancing their homes to accomplish the same end, but with $100 to $300 in costs. The high absolute total cost of this longterm borrowing is ignored. Those who borrow longterm money to buy furniture and automobiles perhaps overlook the fact that they will be paying interest on the loan long after the furniture and cars have been junked. The interest cost will be several times greater than a conventional installment loan, but this is of no concern, for the art of *debtizing* is concerned only with the size of the current payments.

To the borrower, his mortgage term is so long that it seems as if it will never be repaid during his lifetime anyway, or at least during his period of ownership, so he convinces himself that he might just as well take advantage of this new-fangled windfall. Often he looks to his life insurance as the only way to shed the longterm mortgage, so why should he worry about paying it off—or for that matter, extending it a few more years. At various times during the long boom, savings institutions and banks have actively promoted refinancing of this type.

Until 1957, construction and mortgage totals were about equal each year, but during the sixties the yearly mortgage figures have been outstripping the construction figures by growing amounts with a sharp speed-up beginning in 1961. The National Industrial Conference Board estimated as far back as 1963 that the formation of new mortgages exceeded the value of construction of one to four-family homes by $10 billion.

Another lending practice that may someday receive closer scrutiny is the inclusion of appliances and carpeting in the appraisal of a house on which a longterm mortgage is issued (thirty years, for example). Not only will these appliances and carpeting be rendered useless long before the mortgage is satisfied, but the total cost of financing them in this manner is very high. There is little difference between refinancing or extending a mortgage to buy a refrigerator and dishwasher and including them in the original financing.

Land prices, fed by much credit, continued to rise throughout the great boom. Lenders feel more secure when holding high ratio mortgages. They also have allowed borrowers to receive even more cash than their mortgage reduction when refinancing. Builders were reported promoting intriguing financing plans which project the increase in property values. When the first mortgage commitment is insufficient for the buyer because he lacks the difference between it and the purchase price, the builder takes a short-term, low installment, "balloon" second mortgage. The "balloon" note is not fully amortized so that when it matures, there is still a balance due. The builder tells the buyers that in three or four years, whenever the "balloon" second mortgage is due—and often this final payment amounts to several thuosand dollars—the rise in land values together with the intervening reduction of the first mortgage will permit the first mortgage to be refinanced or extended, thus supplying the funds necessary to satisfy this second mortgage. The pitfalls in this process are evident to all who care to look. What if property values were to decline and the borrower could not raise the thousands of dollars necessary to satisfy the then due second mortgage?

MORTGAGE DEBT INFLUENCES BOOM

The institutions of the mortgage lending field have been augmented, modified, and enlarged greatly. This has not been mere coincidence and these changes have been responsible in no small way for the expansion. Accompanying these structural changes has been a continually evolving attitude toward such debt, and some remarkable practices in dealing with it which together have worked to generate an astronomical mortgage debt. The size of this debt by itself is not cause for great concern but some of the practices, attitudes, and methods employed' in handling it should be.

The institution of "home ownership" is highly desirable. It seems to provide an inner security. It develops an amazing concern on the part of the occupants for the wellbeing of the structure in which they reside. It is conducive to a better overall standard of living.

On the negative side, human frailty has contributed to the perversion of mortgage lending principles. The evils of this probably will be felt indirectly by savers and their lending institutions, while all the citizens through federal guaranteed loans could bear the burden of their blunders. Far more tragic will be the personal disasters which may be borne by the families directly involved. Also, an adverse product of the easy mortgage credit is the "unsupervised renter." This is the family that occupies a home to which they have title, but in which they have little or no equity or interest. These people are really renters in attitude who, if not indeed, occupy a house while allowing it to deteriorate until it becomes so bad that even they can no longer tolerate it—whereupon they abandon it to the mortgagee. In the case of the FHA insured loan the house becomes a dubious federal asset.

A situation with which we have had little experience under difficult economic conditions is the larger fixed personal expenses associated with the over-extension of mortgage and consumer credit. It is reasonable to assume that because of the priority given to mortgage payments, any significant decline in disposable income would result in a drastic change in spending patterns, the consequences of which could be far reaching.

We have been experiencing a fabulous trend in housing. Comparing the nature of the housing built twenty years ago with that built today reveals a spectacular rise in living standards, and to extend this trend through several decades would challenge the imagination of a science fiction writer. This is particularly true when contemplating the debt structure that would be necessary to pay for it.

The institutions and practices devised to generate this vast mortgage debt have been so effective that a large part of our productive capacity has become dependent upon them. A continuation of the trend and a further liberalizing of mortgage credit would be to invite disaster particularly if more instability in the economy is generated by bad money management.

Lending practices in this area should be permitted to be stabilized in relation to the rest of the economy. It takes only an occasional reminder in the form of economic adjustment for a lending institution to repent and to abandon whatever unsound lending practices it may have engaged in. The reminders are essential to keep them on the right track. Federal efforts to forestall the economic adjustment encourages greater and greater abandonment of sound lending practices, the consequence of which is a weakened debt structure. Occasional minor economic adjustments, therefore, work to prevent the excesses that could lead to economic chaos.

CONCLUSION

The mortgage on the homestead has, over recent years, lost its preferred position. It has been comingled with other borrowings to enable frivolous consumption and stock speculation. The easy availability of mortgage money has frequently lessened respect for the commitment.

All of this notwithstanding, home ownership, made possible in the majority of cases only by virtue of the mortgage credit innovations, has created a vast comfortable housing structure which for the most part is a pampered child. The billions of man hours and billions of dollars spent improving, preserving and protecting this housing structure would be beyond the comprehension of socialist housing bureaucrats. Human nature is such that ownership generates a vastly different attitude toward a residence than when it is rented.

The many credit innovations have funneled vast sums into housing. This availability of credit combined with the long-term amortized loan has produced sufficient "loose linkage" which has permitted land and interest costs to become disproportionately high as they compare to the incomes of average families. Credit is not unlimited, and housing will have to share the available capital with business, municipalities and other users. Further schemes to divert more funds to housing will come only at the expense of the other users.

The interests of savers cannot be trampled if sufficient funds are to be available for mortgage loans. Lenders cannot be robbed by inflation year after year to an even greater degree, and our credit institutions thrive. Stability is essential to healthy mortgage credit institutions and healthy mortgage credit institutions are essential to a healthy economy. The governmental policies generating successive periods of excessive stimulation and retardation have created as unhealthy a climate for savers and investors as rational minds should care to contemplate. Hopefully the seventies will see stability restored to the economy with a diminished rate of inflation and a steady and sustainable rate of growth.

FOOTNOTES

1. J. E. Morton. **Urban Mortgage Lending: Comparative Markets and Experience,** a Study by the National Bureau of Economic Research, New York. Princeton, N. J.: Princeton University Press, 1956, p. 100.

2. From the Federal Reserve Bulletins.

3. James S. Duesenberry, **Business Cycles and Economic Growth.** New York, N. Y.: McGraw-Hill Book Co. Inc., 1958, p. 165.

4. Duesenberry, **pg.** 138.

5. Ibid, **pg.** 164.

6. "Danger Signals Show Up in Credit." **Business Week,** March 16, 1963.

7. Lawrence G. O'Donnell. **The Wall Street Journal,** Jan. 21, 1965.

inflation : more money in system than goods.
easy credit causes higher int rates

79

Chapter VII

JUST ONE MORE

Private ownership of the productive resources of our economy, shared by virtually anyone who cares to participate, is the keystone of modern capitalism. This ownership ranges from the small businessman who operates a proprietorship form of business to the massive corporations, whose ownership is spread over the entire free world economy and is held by millions of individuals.

The proprietor or small businessman always knows the value of his assets. He is well aware of what they are able to produce and he is in constant contact with them physically. On the other hand, the shareholders of a large corporation often know nothing of the productive assets due to the flexibility of accounting procedures.

Therefore, these remote stockholders look to the price of their shares as a measure of how well their investment is doing, rather than to the productive assets, the earnings or the dividends paid by the corporation. It is easy for the shareholders to reason that in spite of what is happening to earnings or dividends, if the price of the stock is rising, they are doing well. It is this elasticity, if you will, between the actual development of the business and the price of the shares that has produced a situation in which the wise appear foolish and the foolish appear wise. It provides a situation that appears at times to produce "instant wealth." It has generated income by the sheer manipulation of numbers. With such a potential, it is little wonder that all manner of schemes and financial fantasies have been indulged.

The businessman has not escaped the temptation of self-deception. As a shareholder of his publicly-traded corporation, he too, has been tempted to appraise the success of his business in terms of the price of its shares, his knowledge of the intrinsic value of the corporation notwithstanding. This businessman's obsession with the price of the shares of his corporation has led to all manner of perverse financial and accounting arrangements.

People in government also have been deluded by this stock price fallacy and have permitted it to influence their decisions on behalf of government and governmental agencies. As with most such errors, it will probably be asked in retrospect, "How could such intelligent people be enticed to commit such gross errors of judgment?" It is to the exploration of the cause of these errors of judgment by individuals, businessmen, and government officials and some of the consequences thereof that this chapter is directed.

MASS SELF-DECEPTION

Because the 1929 stock market crash was followed by the great and protracted depression, many, or perhaps most people reasoned that the latter was attributable to the first. We are, in recent years, realizing that the "great depression" was the result of forces other than the stock market, probably the incredible shrinkage of the supply of money.

In nearly all discussions of the great crash, it is stated that the stock owners were "on 10 percent margin" and implied that all or nearly all were. Why 10 percent? Was that the lowest? No, some had worked out ways to trade wthout putting up any money at all. As a matter of practice, however, firms commonly required fifty percent of the purchase price. But all of that notwithstanding, stock prices had regained most of the losses by the spring of 1930. People confuse the stock prices of 1932 with the crash, while, in fact, they were two different markets. By 1932 even the many people who had owned the stock outright had to sell in that grossest liquidity crisis.

Out of the confusion of the hearings and inquests came a unanimous verdict, "guilty!" Stock market credit was condemned and it was sentenced to the whimsical and interminable manipulation of the Fed. This provided a fetish that is believed by the cult of equities to keep the threat of a stock market panic from their abode.

The fact is that such credit controls are ill-applied and ineffectual. The Fed has applied them although not as the Congress had intended "for the purpose of preventing the excessive use of credit for the purchase and carrying of securities . . .", but in a manner that is consistent with attempts to affect stock trading. An examination of stock market credit in the record-breaking bull market of the fifties and sixties reveals some interesting facts. The amount of credit has risen in stair-step fashion from less than $1 billion in 1949 to about $10 billion in 1968. In 1949, the margin requirements were 75 percent, and in 1969 they were 80 percent (at 80 percent margin, only 20 percent can be borrowed.)

There has been virtually no correlation between the amount of credit and the various levels of margin requirements during the rising market. During those twenty years, the margin requirements were changed twelve times: They were raised on January 17, 1951, from 50 percent to 75 percent with customer debit balances—loans by brokers—at the $1.3 billion level. On January 16, 1958, they were lowered from 70 percent to 50 percent—this with debit balances at the $2.5 billion level. In 1955, the margin requirements were raised twice, changing the minimums from 50 percent to 70 percent, this with debit balances at the $2.5 billion level. In 1960, they were lowered again with loans at the $3 billion level. Again they were lowered on July 10, 1962, with loans at the $3.5 billion level. In 1963 they were raised from 50 percent to 70 percent with debit balances under $6 billion and lowered in 1970 from 80 to 65 percent, with balances over $6 billion.

There is little correlation with the level of credit, but there is a good correlation between the level of stock prices and the margin requirements. This suggests that the authority had during this period applied its great wisdom in an effort to manipulate the stock market, rather than to control the quantity of credit, as the act granting this power required. The restriction on stock market credit serves little practical purpose other than perhaps to mitigate the adverse effects on the stock market of the Fed's transgressions in money management—a matter to which the Fed could have better allocated the time and effort spent on margin requirements. This is especially true in today's market which is dominated by institutional activity functioning without leverage (borrowed money).

For the people interested in borrowing more than the margin requirements on their stock, circumvention of the "margin requirements" has been simple. Upon approaching their banker for a collateral loan, they needed only state that they intended to use the money for some purpose other than purchasing more stock which actually may be the case when one considers how family funds are mixed.

Not too many years ago, the mortgaging of one's home to "play the stock market" would have been considered foolhardy by most. Even today, such a deliberate act would be viewed with skepticism, but the fact is that there are millions of families who own stock today by virtue of a home mortgage loan. It is just that the loan was not specifically arranged to buy stock, and for this reason, the two transactions are not thought of as being related to each other. Family finances have become so comingled, however, that in fact, the separation of the mortgage from the stock purchase makes no difference. If a family has a twenty thousand dollar mortgage on the house and has purchased ten thousand dollars worth of stock, don't they own the stock by virtue of the mortgage loan? If there is a question about this, we need only ask: which—the stock or the home—is likely to be sold

84

if one or the other has to be liquidated? The same can be said for most stock collateral loans.

THE MISQUOTES

The stock market is a generator of income and optimism. Essential to a discussion of the stock market as an income generator is an exposure of the "nebulous stock market dollar." Most equity evaluations are difficult, but in the minds of those who follow the market quotations the mechanics of the market have made them extremely easy.

It starts quite innocently as an arithmetical exercise at the breakfast table. By merely looking up the last trade of the previous day in one's stock in the morning financial page and multiplying that price by the number of shares held, one can determine almost at an instant, the "exact" worth of the certificate owned. This "bank-book accounting" of equity values is so broadly practiced, it has far-reaching effects.

The fact is that this price was received by someone else and only applies to him. It should be of substantially less concern to the stock owners. All of the shareholders should not assume that they could liquidate at the same price for this would be absurd. Actually, equity values are far more nebulous than these exact and simple measurements indicate. The thought that two parties through their broker, when agreeing to trade 100 shares of General Motors at one-half dollar per share below the previous transaction, can destroy almost $150 million of value is incredible.[1] Certainly, these people are not responsible for any such theft from their fellows, but under the precise accounting that prevails it becomes a sizeable larceny. Conversely, the same parties agreeing on a price one-half dollar higher, could bring glee to many hundreds of thousands of G.M. stock owners that practice this accounting. The practice is reinforced by governmental authorities such as Internal Revenue, who employing this appraisal method, arrive at a figure so wonderfully accurate to the last penny. Even in the political promotions of 1964, for example, it was pointed out by a leading columnist that from November of 1963 to July, 1964, stock values had increased by $100 billion. At best, such a figure could only be considered some sort of happiness quotient. News media, in reporting stock price declines, will often state dramatically how many billions of dollars of value have been lost.

Moreover, stock owners who have so accurately calculated their worth, seldom, if ever, allow for capital gains tax. If a person had paid the equivalent of $10.00 per share for General Motors and the price of the last transaction is $100.00, he sees himself worth the larger figure, and to liquidate means "giving away" so many dollars in income tax. The capital gains tax combined with these continuous and precise calculations of worth, prevent many people from liquidating stock. As a result, the supply of stock is often restricted and prices are higher and less realistic than they might otherwise be.

Realistically speaking, the price of the last transaction in a stock belongs only to the parties involved. The rest of the shareholders of that issue will most likely take some other price, if they sell at all. The idea that equities can be so precisely appraised is indeed fallacious.

Broad boundary appraisals of stock by individuals, institutions, and government would allow a more realistic and flexible approach to the stock market. It might arrest some of the excitement of a boom and reduce concern in the panic, lessening the magnitude of both.

The stock market becomes an immense impersonal machine. People buy stock "from" it and people sell stock "to" it. If they buy a stock that rises in price, it seldom occurs to them that someone else sold the stock and missed the rise. Conversely, if they sell a stock at a high price and it goes down, the pleasure is not diminished by any consideration for the unknown party who bought their stock and is suffering the loss. One speculator told a sad tale of a stock he had purchased at $10.00 and sold at $40.00—which subsequently went to $60.00. He said, "Look at the money I lost." But he shed no crocodile tears for the person who sold it to him for $10.00 or gave a thought to what he had "lost." Buying and selling stock is seldom thought of as a contest between individuals; the idea is that you just beat the numbers.

STOCKS GENERATE INCOME

The cliche about "putting money in the market" is so widely used, it is accepted literally by many. More accurately, the saying should be "putting money through the market." If savings are used to purchase stock, part is converted to commissions, part goes to taxes, and the proceeds end up as a credit to someone's account. Nothing remains in the market but a new bid or asking price! A part of the proceeds might often be capital gains in a prolonged rising market. This income is no different than that obtained from the sale of real estate at a profit. This income, which becomes such for income tax purposes by virtue of the transaction, is often spent. It is easy to see, therefore, how a rising stock market becomes an "income generator." Savings and money borrowed from the banking system are converted to income by the market. The Mutual Fund industry, which was conceived in the twenties, has grown to a significant size in the last twenty years, and has become a systematic converter of capital gains to income. Competition among the funds makes the annual realization and distribution of capital gains essential to the contentment of shareholders.

Like the magician who keeps pouring water from the pitcher, yet the pitcher remains full—the question might be asked, "How can savings be converted to taxes, commissions, and profit-income by the market and still appear to be intact?" The answer is found in accounting. As the savings pass through the market, the residual price tends to rise. Now, multiply the new price by the shares outstanding, as is the custom, and you will find that in spite of the conversion, the overall savings appear to be either intact or appreciated. Let us say for purposes of illustration that a stock owner decides to spend some of his "paper profits" for a new boat. He sells some of his shares to another individual who uses savings and a bank loan to pay for them. The seller pays his commission, sets aside some of the proceeds for the income tax liability the sale created, and with the remainder, pays for the boat. The only thing left in the market during a period of optimism is a higher price level of trading. As prices rise, the "value" of the sellers remaining shares may soon equal the amount he had before the purchase of the boat. The buyer is happy because by practicing "financial page accounting," he now has more than the amount of the savings and bank money used to purchase the stock. And his savings and the proceeds of his collateral loan have been spent by the seller, by the brokers, and yes, by Uncle Sam.

The price remains the equilibrium level of supply and demand and has no direct, quantitative relationship to the amount of savings or borrowed money invested. The rising prices conceal the fact that savings and borrowed money have been converted to income, as it appears that all are intact, if not "appreciated." A rapidly declining market shows us quite vividly that the equilibrium price can be revised downward quickly, thus demonstrating the complete independence of the price and the quantity of monies involved. A fifteen or twenty percent decline in the price of a stock can occur in minutes with the trading of relatively few shares and with a relatively small dollar amount. When these lower prices are multiplied by the vast number of shares outstanding, it becomes apparent that the dollar amount of trading activity has no direct bearing on changes in the value of outstanding shares. It is this fact that conceals from view the conversion to income of savings placed in common stock. Also, failure to understand this makes the nebulousness of equity appraisals elusive to most people.

Unrealized capital gains tend to have an effect on spending. Having calculated their improved net worth, people feel affluent and are more inclined to spend. And it should be kept in mind that the converse of this is also true. A friend about to leave to spend the summer in Europe told me that he had lost over a hundred thousand dollars in liquidating value in the previous six months and that if he hadn't already paid for the trip, he wouldn't go. Even though his income was unaffected, he would not have made the trip because of the decline in current liquidating value.

When companies turn to the equity market to raise capital for expansion, virtually all the monies raised are thus converted into income. Savings and borrowed monies flow directly to investment—in most cases, expenditures for plant and equipment. This function is most predominant in periods of high stock prices. Companies occasionally see common stock as the cheapest way to raise money, particularly when stock sells at high "times earnings ratios" and low yields. When stock prices are low, the amounts of new common stock offerings are extremely restricted. As the boom grows older, speculation grows popular, and booming stock markets become substantial contributors to the boom, both directly and psychologically.

Rising stock prices reach beyond those directly affected by them—the investors, speculators, brokers, and the companies whose stock is traded. As we have shown, a bull market enables and encourages greater spending by those who participate. This, in turn, affects households that have no contact with and little knowledge of the markets. Also, businessmen whose personal fortunes have been enhanced by the rising stock prices tend to be bouyant and optimistic. This exuberance follows them to work where a sense of wellbeing can contribute to an affimative decision about investment for expansion, improvements, or adding leverage to the companies' capital structure. Such investment decisions can affect the lives of people far out of touch with this world of finance.

A PERSPECTIVE

For over 20 years following the 1929 stock market crash, writers were still delving into why people could commit such gross errors of judgment. Most of what they had to say about the bull market preceding the 1929 crash can be said about the wild speculative binge of 1967-1968. There were, however, a few distinguishing elements that came into play in the market of the 1960's. Some of the financial wizardry of the 1960's was but a mere twist to the old practice of the 20's of pyramiding public utility companies through the public utility holding company, but we will deal with that later.

The wild speculative market of 1967-68 did not just happen. Exuberance in the stock market was the product of world factors and events that preceded this time. In order to put it all into perspective, let us go back to the previous time when the stock market was witnessing the rampant overenthusiasm of a bull market—1929.

Stock markets that are overly enthusiastic and optimistic are subject to a very rapid "sell off." The enthusiasm and activity are based upon numbers, and if the numbers start to move in the other direction, they have to fall a long way to reach a point where the earnings and dividends justify the price. The emotionalism tends to work in both directions as well, and it is reasonable to anticipate that stock prices will be as depressed as they were previously inflated. In the fall of 1929, the bull market terminated, a sell-off occurred, and stock prices dropped about one-half, but by the spring of 1930 they had recovered over half of the losses and stock prices were not too far from what they had been a year earlier. It was the subsequent deterioration of the economy which continued in the last half of 1930, in 1931 and 1932, that was the matrix of the protracted bear market of those years. The stock market crash of 1929 did not crush people's faith in the stock market, but the following two years did. But pessimism is no more permanent than optimism. By 1937, stock market prices had rallied substantially. The recession or depression of 1937-1938, however, combined with ensuing war years, snuffed out this spark of interest in the stock market, so that by the late 1940's, the stock market had very little following and very few friends. But starting about 1949, interest in the stock market began to increase. It increased almost steadily over the 20 years that followed. Price earnings ratios in 1949 were commonly 7 or 8 times earnings, and with the exception of only minor interruptions, these price earnings multiples continued to become higher and higher until the late 60's, when the stocks that were capable of capturing the imagination of the public were selling at multiples of 30, 40 and 50 times earnings and higher. There were intervals during this 20-year span that saw some weak and even panicky sell-offs in the market. The most severe of these were in 1957, 1962, and 1966, but each time the market seemed to return to a new, higher level of enthusiasm and speculation. Such events merely caused the investors to become less and less timid, relying on their experience that the following year prices would come back and the interest in common stock would be even greater.

Growing in concert with this long bull market had been the ability and the facilities for merchandising stock. Communications equipment designed for and allocated to stock markets had, in this 20-year period, changed from the use of the 600 digit per minute stock ticker and translux projector, which were used in combination with large chalk boards, to computer read-out devices that provide the user with the up to the minute information on the trading of thousands and thousands of issues. The sales forces mustered to sell common stock, as well as mutual funds shares, had grown fantastically in this period. So as we look back, we see the higher quality common stocks fairly accurately measured by the Dow-Jones Industrial Averages, going from a time in 1949, when they sold 7½ or 8 times earnings, to a time in 1961, when they sold for about 24 times earnings. Their excesses were corrected in 1962 as the market sell-off took the form of a true panic. To evaluate what followed in the 60's, it is necessary to look at the philosophy of government. Coming into full bloom with the Kennedy administration was the almost universal acceptance and implementation of Keynesian type theories and theories of the fiscal schools of economics. This led the government to implement policies whose consequences were increasing federal deficit financed by an ever increasing expansion of the money supply. This, coming as it did, at the heels of some 10 to 12 years of advancing stock prices, set the stage for recovery from the 1962 sell-off and the eventual bull market, culminating in February of 1966. At that time, the Federal Reserve, evidently influenced by rising stock prices and inflation, implemented a policy of restraint. And the stock market sell-off of 1966 occurred, as well as a turn down in the growth rate of business activity, in the last quarter of 1966 and the first quarter of 1967.

THE 1967-68 SPECULATIVE BINGE SHOULD NEVER HAVE HAPPENED

On January 1, 1967, Lyndon Johnson was faced with the possibility of a recession occurring during the last two years of his first full term in office. The following occurred:

The costs of the war were intensified and the prospects were for a vastly increased federal deficit if taxes were not increased. He not only did not ask for an increase in taxes in the State of the Union Message of 1967, but the magnitude of the costs of the war were not revealed to the public. He was armed with his recollection of the experiences of the Roosevelt administration and how, in financing of World War II through the expansion of the money supply, the economy swelled to its absolute limits. The nation, still in the grips of Keynesian thinking, was amenable to policies of further deficit financing which disregarded the effect on the money supply. The result of all of this was a massive federal deficit, developing to 28 billion dollars in the first nine months of the fiscal year which began July 1, 1967. To finance this colossal deficit during an economic boom, the Fed was left with the choice of either expanding the money supply, or completely starving the private sector of available funds. This really was no choice at all, and the Federal Reserve, evidently still operating with the belief that changes in the growth rate of money were not too important, expanded the money supply some 17 billion dollars just to accommodate this financing. But slowly we are learning that if you print 17 billion additional dollars and distribute them throughout the nation, business activity will not only go to capacity, but it will be accompanied by inflation. The economic adjustments which had started in the last quarter of 1966 and the first quarter of 1967 were aborted. This, occurring as it did after 18 years of a bull market, fanned the flames of excesses. Of the many words of John Kenneth Galbraith's that Lyndon Johnson heeded, he certainly didn't overlook those that admonish the politician about killing a boom and being identified as the executioner.[2] From this, we should learn that any government can buy an extension to a boom by increasing the rate of expansion of the money supply.

The ensuing spree in the stock market was dominated by speculative issues, causing them to attain prices that could not be related to anything the companies had done or had prospect of ever doing. The investor was hopelessly trapped. The rapid rise in the quantity of money had precipitated an accelerating inflation, as well as driving interest rates to heights and bond prices to depths not witnessed for over 100 years.

Cash was depreciating at an ever faster rate. It seemed only logical to further project a 20-year trend of rising stock prices. The frenzied clamor to ride this road to rapid wealth captured the imagination of virtually the whole nation. The volume of trading rose to such a consistently high level that the brokerage firms became buried in paperwork. The demand for new, unseasoned issues intensified as issue after issue doubled or tripled shortly after being offered to the public.

The time and climate was right for a new generation of financial wizards. The conglomerate assumed the role in the 1960's that the public utility holding companies had assumed in the late 1920's. They did so by merging companies of low price earnings multiples into companies of high price earnings multiples, by exchanging debt securities for equity securities, by liberalizing depreciation, and other accounting procedures. The directors of this new financial alchemy were able to develop corporations with rapidly rising "earnings." This caught the fancy of the investing public, raising even higher the price of the shares which they would offer as an exchange to new candidates for merger.

These excesses and economic distortions need not have occurred if Congress had been truly informed of the rising costs of the war and other federal programs and had raised the taxes to pay for them. For the President to come before the Congress in January of 1968 and recommend a raise in taxes is to lock the barn door after the horse has gone. That plea for fiscal responsibility rang rather hollow.

There are many facts of life about the capitalistic system or any economic system for that matter, that cater to the wishes of consumers. One is that in such a system, economic changes tend to overshoot their mark. The consequence is the affliction of a period of adjustment. The stock market is no exception. It too tends to overshoot. Because economic movement is a result of thousands, or perhaps millions of individual economic decisions, the very natural human error is to project the trend and this is the force behind the "missing of the mark." The injection of the government, reflecting very human motives, run by very human people, does not mitigate this tendency. As the record suggests, it is only exaggerated. The moves of the Johnson Administration in 1967 and 1968 to abort any form of economic adjustment in that period caused the stock market to move into a phase of a bull market that became one of the most wildly speculative binges in the history of this nation.

By 1966, after 17 years of this bull market, there was no place for the market to go and no way to respond to added stimulation. Bull markets tend to become more and more speculative as they get older. To prolong their life is to cause them to become wilder and more unstable. It is just mechanically impossible to have a perpetual bull market because of its continually changing character. This may be no real revelation, but in 1966, the majority opinion was that we had mastered the economy and the perpetual boom was ours, or at least closely within our grasp. There is nothing in our economic system, outside the influence of government, that leads one to believe that it is grossly and inherently unstable. Great deviations from a normal growth pattern of our economy can almost always be traced to government or its management of money. The common stock investor loves stability, i.e. if stability is defined as a never-ending, constantly rising bull market. The bull market, however, is the epitome of instability, and instability is a two-edged sword. It is only in a bear market, after stock prices have declined for some period, that the investor cries for help, and asks for the federal government to do something about the mess and to inject "stability" into the situation. It was the government policy of 1967-68 that so grossly destabilized the market. This unstabilizing governmental policy brought few criticisms for was it not contributing to a glorious, free-wheeling boom? Who in the world could be against prosperity?

John Kenneth Gailbrath wrote, "Since speculative collapse can only follow a speculative boom, one might expect that Wall Street would lay a heavy hand on the resurgence of speculation. The Federal Reserve would be asked by bankers and brokers to lift margins to the limit; it would be warned to enforce the requirement sternly against those who might try to borrow on their own stocks and bonds in order to buy more of them." Further on he added that, while all this might be logically expected . . . it might not come to pass."[3] Indeed, this later judgment has been the correct one. Going back to what we said about some of the facts of life, it is a fact of life that man will always act in his short-sighted self-interest, and it would be unrealistic for anyone to believe that he would act otherwise. Therefore it would be foolish to believe that bankers and brokers would act to limit their own success and thus this *could not* "logically be expected." It is plainly contrary to human nature. By the same token, politicians also can be expected to act in their own shortsighted self-interest. They too, are only human. The 1967-68 experience is consistent with this belief. For these reasons we should not look to government to manipulate the economy as does Professor Galbraith. Quite ironically, the speculative boom that Professor Galbraith suggested should be curbed by bankers and brokers was carved by governmental manipulation to which he was at the very least, a contributing designer.

FOOTNOTES

1. There are some 287,000,000 shares of General Motors outstanding.

2. John K. Galbraith, **The Great Crash of 1929,** Boston. Houghton Mifflin Co., 1955, p. 196.

3. Ibid p. 200.

Chapter VIII

THE BUSINESSMAN'S COCKTAIL

Traditionally, business investment and the resulting debt have been held out as the most fundamental factors of economic expansion. Many explanations of the "business cycle" found in the economics textbooks pivot on these factors. Prior to World War II, business investment was by far the greatest variable, responsible for the largest category of debt, and consequently, thought to be the most influential factor in the expansions and contractions in the economy. Business outlays for capital goods and inventory were not challenged about their size by either federal deficits or consumer and mortgage debt. It is no wonder that economists, prior to this new credit era, gave business investment such exclusive responsibility for good times and held it so liable for the bad times.

It is interesting to note that of all the federal credit programs typifying recent times, none has been of much importance in the business sector. In a study for the "Commission on Money and Credit" it was reported that, "Flows of federal credit into the business sector have been very much smaller than into agriculture or housing and minute in relation to other sources of credit utilized by business."[1]

Many inventions such as computers have revolutionized business procedures and at an accelerating rate. They have been amazing in their feats. So spectacular have been their accomplishments that competition and the quickening pace of business have made them an urgent necessity. They are, indeed, costly and much credit has been arranged to finance their purchase. Big companies have installed the largest computers and smaller companies have installed the largest computers they could afford. Costs that were largely labor before the computer were, when replaced by the electronic equipment, converted to debt service. Segments of business that in earlier periods required little capital, today, because of advances in office equipment, require large capital investment. The computer has made possible the use of other automated equipment which is often elaborate and expensive. Like the computer in the office, these new, self-sufficient machines have caused labor costs to be converted to debt service and depreciation.

Earlier periods of prosperity have been attributed to the development of industries that require large amounts of capital. Highly capital-intensive railroads had a great and prolonged effect on our country's development and growth. The street railway systems and the electric utilities also were earlier users of savings. The electric and the telephone utility development has carried right on into and through the current expansion. The incredible number and variety of electrical appliances that have been conceived in recent decades have taxed the capacities of electric utility companies. Vast capital outlays have been necessary for the increased production of this electricity. Because of the stability of earnings and the monopolistic character of the electric utilities, about one half of the funds required have been raised by borrowing. The same can be said of the telephone utilities. Few industries have ever developed that are so well suited for bearing debt.

After World War II, another very capital intensive industry began to assume a position of prominence—the natural gas transmission and distribution industry. Natural gas, which in earlier days was often a bothersome by-product of oil production, is now collected and piped to distant points for consumption. This not only created an immense network of pipelines which supply virtually the whole country, but it revitalized the declining gas distribution systems. This, too, has been done with highly leveraged capital structures —large amounts of bonded indebtedness.

100

The airlines comprise another industry that has borrowed extensively to finance the large investment in costly jet airplanes. The cost of a modern jet airliner so dwarfs the cost of earlier aircraft that the greatest impact of these investments has been felt only in the most recent years.

Many industries' sales or gross revenues vary quite directly with consumer incomes or the income of other businesses. When they are in a period of heavy capital outlays themselves, they contribute to their own demand. Certainly, as a result of the large sums of money spent by the airlines to purchase planes, many additional passenger miles are made possible, if not required. This is an important element of any expansion. The future holds the promise that capital investments are unlimited. Let's hope that in any future periods of slack in the economy the old invalid idea that there isn't enough investment demand to employ available savings does not reappear.

The service industries, because of rising disposable incomes, enjoyed rapid growth during the boom. The increased income has been spent on goods and services with a lower priority on the list of consumer "needs." The restaurant business has, for example, had many more dollars spent with it as larger incomes have allowed more people to enjoy the luxury of eating out. Restaurants, too, have been responsible for substantial capital investments. The ready availability of mortgage money for their construction and financing of the equipment has made possible the proliferation of restaurants to meet this demand.

DURATION OF PROSPERITY AFFECTS BUSINESS SPENDING AND BORROWING

The duration of the expansion was extensive which, in turn, affected business decisions about future capital requirements and thus, current capital expenditures. "If income rises steadily for a number of years, managements will develop a strong tendency to project that growth rate into the future. But if incomes fluctuate about an upward trend, the tendency to project the trend into the future will be greatly weakened."[2] Prolonged good times breed over-optimism which simultaneously feeds the prosperity while threatening its very existence. The efforts of the federal government to sustain and extend an uninterrupted expansion by means of budgetary deficits and expansion of money to finance them contributed to the tendency of management to misjudge long-term requirements and make over-optimistic projections.

It is easy to see how, in this segment of the economy, the cumulative effects of expansion come into play. Because of the pleasant nature of expansion, there is little concern about tendencies to over-expand. It is acutely hoped during an expansion that no such excesses exist or will ever become apparent.

The extensive utilization of debt in other areas by the consumers, municipalities and the federal government and expansion of the money in response to these credit demands forced industry to operate at near capacity. This, in turn, caused industry to expand its capability to meet the credit-inflated demand. The industrial executives must determine how the new plants and equipment will be paid for.

The monies come primarily from five basic sources. They come internally from depreciation and retained earnings—earnings not distributed as dividends. Externally, they come from the issuance and sale of bonds, stocks, or from banks. The factors governing which types and what combination to use to raise the required funds are seldom simple.

Notwithstanding the multiplicity of considerations, there was a tendency for corporations to turn more to the issuance of debt obligations. Debt accelerates the decline of net income of a business in bad times, and accelerates the rise of net earnings during an economic expansion. It follows that when new funds are needed, businessmen functioning under the optimistic conditions of a boom would choose a route that would accelerate their success. After already accepting as "given" a bright expansionistic future which is implicit in the first decision to expand, it is quite natural that they should borrow the money, leverage their capital structure, and realize greater net profits.

Today an executive with thirty years experience has witnessed only expansion with few minor exceptions. The generation that had to deal with the problems of the thirties has for the most part been retired. A whole generation of businessmen have risen to important positions; men who have never witnessed in their business experience a major contraction. Even for those business managers who had experienced the troubled times, the long, long expansion lessened their fears. It should be no surprise then, that less and less consideration was given to defense against hard times. In the middle sixties, one reporter put it this way, "Like the consumers they sell to, U.S. corporations are plunging deeply into debt to buy the things they want in this era of prosperity." "In their case," he goes on, "the borrowed money is often long-term—taking the form of a mounting flood of corporate bonds."[3]

Corporate borrowing reached unprecedented levels, such borrowing occurring when internal sources fail to supply the funds for the desired expansion. Commitment to capital expansion maturing at a time of internal financial strain, forced many corporations into the capital markets at inopportune times.

The rush to expand capacity through debt financing came, as usual, at a time when the production capacity was already highly employed. The new urgency for more tools and equipment pressed still harder against the capacity, making even more urgent the need.

An interesting note regarding the manner in which corporations have been borrowing large sums of money in the recent boom years is the growing trend toward placing the whole bond issue with one or a small group of large institutions. This is known as private placement and is contrasted

103

with the traditional public bond offering. Such private placements had a rapid rise in the early 1960's. This can be attributed not only to the great supply of savings available through the rapidly expanding insurance companies and pension funds, but to the lower costs of "selling" the issue and a considerably greater flexibility available to the borrower as to the terms, restrictions, and ability to renegotiate the terms of the debt.

For shorter term money, companies have looked to the banking system. Commercial and industrial loans by the banks doubled in the decade with the heaviest demand developing in the latter years. Needless to say, the accelerating expansion of "newly created" money did its share to feed and nourish the boom.

Depreciation, a major factor in supplying funds and encouraging capital improvements, was allowed to accrue at a faster rate by Congress and the U.S. Treasury Department. In 1954, a law was passed that allowed business to use more rapid methods of depreciation for tax purposes. In 1953 and 1962, the U.S. Treasury made significant efforts to allow more liberal depreciation claims and to shorten the average life guidelines of depreciable facilities which enlarged depreciation allowances. These deductions from corporate earnings provided in some measure a type of "forced" savings that tended to accelerate replacement with more efficient and productive facilities. As business income expanded during the boom, the larger write-off to depreciation had not had too noticeable an effect on net earnings. Only after the economic slow-down of 1969-70, bringing decreased profits, did many corporations change their accounting methods to reduce rates of depreciation in an effort to raise published earnings.

In addition to these provisions, the Congress implemented a seven percent tax credit for certain capital investments. In effect, the company making a capital outlay is allowed a "rebate" in the year of the outlay amounting to seven percent of the cost. This federal subsidy to investment modified the economic efficiency of an investment by increasing its prospective profitableness through a reduction of its cost. This measure heightened federal deficits, encouraged investment, and further fed the boom.

Retained earnings tend to remain a certain percentage of net earnings, at least while they are expanding. This is to say that management often has a policy of raising dividends, so as to maintain a payout at some relatively constant fraction of the increasing net income. For example, many companies have a policy of paying out 50 percent of net income in dividends. Throughout the expansion, dividends overall have increased and reciprocally, the earnings retained have increased. These increasing funds were substantial and since they exceeded the needs for new plants and equipment, managements turned to all manner of financial investments—acquisitions and mergers.

A concentration of business influence and power resulted from the great increase in mergers and acquisitions which in turn are substantially a product of our tax laws. Individuals and families whose assets are considerable and who control corporations realize that greater dividend income for them would only fall subject to the confiscatory personal income tax which currently reaches as high as 70%. It is only reasonable that such business managers would choose not to pay greater dividends to themselves but to retain the earnings through corporate reinvestment.

As we suggested earlier, high stock prices play a role in the movement toward business combination and, in some cases, the reduction of competition. High evaluations of companies in terms of stock prices are also a result of tax law restrictions on the market (we have mentioned the restricting effect on the supply of stock to the market caused by the capital gains tax). Further, the supply of new stock is vastly restricted because of the difference in the effect on earnings, or to put it another way, the cost of financing by the sale of additional stock as opposed to the sale of debt securities. The inclusion of the 48% federal corporate income tax with the cost of obtaining more capital through the sale of stock frequently precludes this course of action.

Inordinately high income taxes have forced all manner of distortions into our system. The encouragement of power concentrations and the reduction of competition in business rank among the worst. People with the determination and the genius to amass fortunes will also master the skills and obtain the talent necessary to circumvent whatever obstacles the Congress may erect. The nation would do better to abandon excessively high income tax rates because circumvention is so remunerative it has become the rule rather than the exception. The costs of having such non-functioning tax laws in order to placate the consciences of some would-be "social engineers" are high in terms of economic dislocation. They are enormous in terms of perversion of business efforts and efficiency, or diminished human incentive and in terms of the misallocation of virtually millions of highly skilled and highly paid attorneys, accountants and others to the task of avoiding excessive taxes.

CONCLUSION

The businessman operates at capacity only with ambivalence. The moment he reaches capacity, he immediately presses hard to expand further thus moving away from a situation of highest efficiency—and often profitability. If most businesses reach capacity simultaneously, they find themselves bidding hard against each other for the means of expanding. The urgency of these projects allow little concern for the rising cost of such construction. The lack of concern is abetted by the fact that the expansion is coincident with highest profits. The compulsion to expand capacity not only causes the higher costs of construction to be discounted, but rising interest rates as well have little or no effect on these decisions.

Governmental mismanagement of its fiscal affairs and the

money of the country forced most businesses into just such a situation with nearly all businesses trying to expand at once. The responsibility for this gross instability can be laid nowhere else.

The consequences are that most businesses wind up with excess capacity at the same time. The excess capacity, though not their intent, is often their destiny for periods of time. Variations of this sequence of events have led students of economics to believe that business investment is a widely fluctuating and inherently unstable part of the economy.

Worry about this "paper tiger" has caused many to believe that government expenditures should be so directed as to counteract it. But our experience has been that government actions have exacerbated the problems. The time lag between the inauguration of a government program designed to counteract an economic condition and the effectiveness of such a program commonly results in the program stimulating the economy during a boom and retarding it during a recession. The overstimulation of the economy during the sixties, the resultant inflation, and the obstacles to business judgment these created set the stage for many business crises and debacles—some of the best known of which were Lockheed, Penn Central, and Goodbody & Co.

Perhaps a stable climate with regard to fiscal and monetary policies would result in business investment working in a more stable manner—with different industries expanding at different times rather than being forced to operate at capacity simultaneously by governmental meddling. Avoidance of government generated distortions in economic activity would make for sounder business judgment while tax reform would free the economy of the loss of billions of highly skilled but unproductive man-hours now allocated to the collection and avoidance of oppressive and complicated taxes.

FOOTNOTES

1. Warren A. Law, Federal Credit Programs, Prentice-Hall, page 283.
2. Duesenberry, p. 214.
3. Wall Street Journal, August 20, 1965, by James E. Bylin, Staff Reporter.

Chapter IX

ONE NEED NOT DRINK ALONE

There are many people who bear no personal debt. However, through the allocation of part of their income to state and local governments via state and local taxes, they can participate as indirect borrowers in a colossal debt structure. By 1969, the average American—man, woman and child—bore $380 in state and local government debt. The heaviest burden rested on New Yorkers ($575), while the lightest was on Arkansans ($220).[1] Collectively we bear more debt than we might be able or care to bear individually. The delegation of these financial decisions to state and local politicians has created some "loose linkage." This has often permitted business and political interests to be served at the expense of the best interests of the taxpayers.

This "collective method" of incurring debt when combined with the exemption from federal income tax granted to the interest paid on such debt, which lowers the interest costs of such borrowing, has increased the communities ability to support greater debt with any given income. The expanding state and local debt has become a significant factor.

The growing and continually moving population exerts a constant pressure on public facilities. Technological advances, too, exert a force that necessitates the replacement and improvement of existing facilities plus completely new facilities which provide services never before available. The constantly increasing density of population resulting from the growth of metropolitan areas has exerted great pressure for ever more costly public facilities.

STATE AND LOCAL GOVERNMENT SECURITY ISSUES

ANNUALLY

BILLIONS OF DOLLARS

Refunding

New capital

20

15

10

5

The Board of Governors of the Federal Reserve System
Historical Chart Book 1971

110

By the middle sixties, schools and colleges were responsible for about 30 percent of the existing debt, while government-owned utilities accounted for 23 percent, and highways for 18 percent.[2]

The great depression, which saw so many of our financial institutions collapse, also saw state and local governments struggle under their debt burden. Being barely able, or at times even unable, to service bonds already outstanding, these governments were in no position to expand their debt regardless of how pressing the need. Just as these troubled waters were about crossed, World War II broke out and there were very few resources to allocate to school and road construction. There were, therefore, fifteen years during which the state and local government debt stood still or declined, while public facilities became less adequate daily. It was to be expected that this would cause a rapid rise in the construction of public facilities once the war was over.

By 1946 much had to be done to make up for the great lack of public facilities. State and local governments were back on their financial feet by the end of the war as revenues had increased substantially. In 1940, their total revenues were $11.7 billion and by 1946, these had increased some 36 percent to $15.9 billion.[3] Meanwhile, the debt through normal and accelerated reduction was becoming a decreasing burden. By the end of World War II, the stage was set for a rapid rise in the volume of public investment.

The inadequacies that had developed because there had been few additions to the school plant during the depression and war years were greatly compounded by the change in family planning that occurred with World War II. The bumper crop of "war babies" soon swelled the school population. School boards for twenty years have raced ahead with plans for school construction, trying to stay ahead of this tidal wave of pupils.

The colleges and universities, whose facilities were made almost hopelessly inadequate in the early post war years as a result of the G.I. benefits, have struggled for a quarter of a century to build sufficient facilities.

111

"We will continue to have municipal improvements as long as we vote for them and will probably always complain about our local taxes,"[4] stated a vice president of the First National Bank of Chicago. Need is apparently the primary determinant of the amount of such debt extensions. The history of bond elections shows little correlation with other factors, as indicated by the following table. It suggests, however, that the proposals for the issuance of such bonds can be influenced by a major war and general prosperity of the nation.

Expanding personal income allows the public a collective attitude of greater abandon when voting on proposed bond issues. Public administrators feel greater freedom from possible public resentment when making proposals and commitments to borrow during a period of rising affluence.

The phenomenal growth in the number of passenger automobiles and trucks has strained the imaginations of state and local officials trying to provide roads sufficient to handle the tremendous traffic load. This great demand placed on public financing can be attributed, at least in part, to liberalization in another area, that of financing consumer credit for automobiles. Certainly, there would be fewer cars and consequently less traffic, had not the term of automobile contracts been extended from twelve to eighteen to twenty-four to thirty-six months.

The phenomenal development of aviation has been another peculiarity of this era. The building of the airport and air terminal facilities which has been so extensive in this post war period has, however, added only a little over one billion dollars to the outstanding local government debt.

By 1960, the momentum of greater and greater capital expenditures by state and local governments thrust us into a period of frenzied expansion. The rapidly rising burden of debt service combined with the growing costs of government to place many municipalities in a perilous financial condition. Entering the seventies in this desperate condition they begged the state legislatures and federal government

112

State and Municipal Bond Election Results

(1926–1971)

Since the year 1926, "THE DAILY BOND BUYER" has been keeping a statistical record of the results of State and municipal bond elections based upon current day to day reports. Summaries of the detailed reports on individual elections are published once each month. The yearly totals presented below were compiled from these data. Approximate percentages of amounts approved and defeated indicate the changing attitude of taxpayers toward the creation of new indebtedness.

	Approved Amount $	%	Defeated Amount $	%
1971	3,142,846,335	35	5,862,362,912	65
1970	5,366,441,359	63	3,194,042,145	37
1969	4,286,542,050	40	6,534,047,453	60
1968	8,686,075,169	54	7,459,875,274	46
1967	7,365,194,080	74	2,549,704,766	26
1966	6,515,833,687	77	1,944,831,423	23
1965	5,611,653,628	73	2,095,491,659	27
1964	5,715,400,806	78	1,582,926,248	22
1963	3,626,886,529	63	2,156,807,833	37
1962	4,263,609,903	70	1,850,443,358	30
1961	2,544,327,858	67	1,263,606,943	33
1960	5,916,951,404	85	1,007,889,410	15
1959	2,752,942,464	72	1,087,633,605	28
1958	3,728,455,966	75	1,263,754,101	25
1957	2,733,435,486	77	806,795,602	23
1956	4,642,488,809	87	665,689,492	13
1955	2,885,666,121	65	1,524,453,871	35
1954	2,781,901,503	84	544,154,550	16
1953	1,851,594,537	83	388,769,450	17
1952	2,383,970,390	84	458,278,500	16
1951	2,249,602,957	88	301,174,640	12
1950	1,537,517,326	76	497,983,399	24
1949	2,217,294,115	84	413,331,290	16
1948	1,449,725,477	69	657,517,250	31
1947	1,870,028,900	92	165,013,750	8
1946	1,923,932,726	87	277,742,348	13
1945	562,406,734	87	87,046,650	13
1944	369,399,622	63	216,254,500	37
1943	48,929,526	49	49,559,000	51
1942	94,638,325	57	71,830,194	43
1941	171,532,546	43	223,640,393	57
1940	155,630,558	62	93,670,643	38
1939	102,855,119	39	163,943,176	61
1938	282,251,298	51	268,258,925	49
1937	165,580,954	40	244,583,610	60
1936	186,603,362	64	106,646,004	36
1935	282,703,638	69	128,503,326	31
1934	268,962,755	60	176,692,931	40
1933	507,121,176	83	105,600,483	17
1932	137,206,642	67	68,679,459	33
1931	474,479,811	78	133,474,369	22
1930	626,059,337	69	280,093,532	31
1929	440,995,944	60	295,386,040	40
1928	783,412,085	59	536,889,610	41
1927	560,714,514	73	211,229,080	27
1926	606,933,170	76	193,184,289	24

The Bond Buyer's Municipal Finance Statistics, Vol. 8, May, 1970, p. 16

113

to bail them out. The excesses were beginning to take their toll and a more sober view of local government was starting to take hold.

TAX EXEMPTION AND STATE AND LOCAL GOVERNMENT DEBT

The debt securities of state and local governments enjoy a peculiarity which has made ample funds available at reduced interest rates. The Internal Revenue Code specifically excludes the interest paid on the obligations of state and local governments. This is consistent with a constitutional doctrine of *reciprocal immunity*. The interest paid on these bonds is, therefore, exempt from corporate and personal federal income tax.

Individuals in high graduated income tax brackets are almost compelled by the high tax to use this tax shield. A person with a high bracket of say, 50 percent, who purchased a municipal bond which yields 6 percent, would have to place his money at 12 percent in taxable securities to obtain the same spendable income. The same applies to businesses in similar tax situations. This feature has resulted in a ready supply of funds at lower interest rates.

The lower interest rates have facilitated the "debtizing" of state and local government income. Lower interest costs allow for more debt to be serviced with any given income.

Nearly one-third of these tax exempt bonds are held by individuals, partnerships, and individual trust accounts. Many of these would otherwise pay taxes well in excess of 50 percent, so the benefits of the tax exempt income far surpasses our 50 percent tax example.

Banks hold some 40 percent of this debt. The high quality of many of these bonds and the tax exemption fit well into the banks' investment requirements, particularly in the short maturities. Most state and local bond issues are arranged so that part of the debt matures each year and is liquidated

114

from the yearly income. The banks generally use the early maturities, while insurance companies generally have been interested in the longer maturities. Over 15 percent of this debt is held by insurance companies.

From this, one can see how individual savings flow directly and also indirectly, through insurance and savings accounts, back into the income stream through salaries and materials purchased for school, highway, sewer, bridge, library and hospital construction. Also, one can see how incomes can swell as a result of bank purchase of these bonds. The percentage of such bond purchases by the banking system has been accelerating in recent years.

Federal credit programs for municipalities and local authorities were not a major factor during this period. The Community Facilities Administration, the Public Housing Administration, and Urban Renewal Administration, contributed considerable color to the state and local economic scenery, but have not yet become a major factor. If past experience is any guide, we can anticipate that they will be broadened and expanded in the future.

A fascinating innovation of state and local credit has been the tax exempt industrial revenue bond. Here the local authority issues bonds for the construction of a plant to be leased by some prearranged business concern. The extent of the security backing the bonds is the lease and credit of the corporation using the facility. In effect then, the government body has supplied its tax exemption to the corporation. The plant, in this way, costs the corporation less than if it had to borrow money for the plant, as its competitors do, without the local government affiliation. The communities use this as a lure to bring industry to their area, often from and at a cost to some other community. This quirk of credit looks noticeably incongruous in our competitive system. It has been, in fact, a federal subsidy encouraging business to locate in a community making such arrangements rather than in those that do not. This is just one more example of governmental muddling by meddling with free markets.

115

Physical factors as well as political factors influence bond financing of public facilities. They prevent or reduce "pay as you go" financing. Some public projects are of such a nature as to make construction from current tax and other revenues virtually impossible.

A new high school cannot be constructed one classroom or unit each year until it is completed. Even with separation of units and multiplicity of buildings that characterize many modern schools, each school needs a minimum of classrooms, an auditorium, a gymnasium, a cafeteria, and so on. So great is the outlay that most school districts can accomplish this only through debt financing.

Electric generating capacity can be economically added only in large units. When a municipality adds to its electrical output and intends to pay for it with revenues from the sale of electricity, bond financing is about the only alternative. Similarly, sewer systems and treatment plants as well as great turnpikes and large bridges require large sums to be available for construction over a relatively short period.

Beyond these physical factors necessitating public bond issues, political considerations frequently seem to prevail, at times conflicting with sound judgment. For the politician desirous of making a mark either for furthering his ambitions for future office or for personal gratification, steel, concrete, and glass seem to be quite a satisfactory vehicle. Construction of facilities also serves as a means of rewarding political supporters, through both financing arrangements and construction contracts. These considerations also help to explain the strong support "urgent" projects get from business leaders often associated with construction, steel, concrete, asphalt, and financial interests. The long run fiscal prudence of any project merits a low position of importance when it conflicts with the immediate success of the politicians or businessmen involved.

116

"Pay as you go" isn't all bad, or at least not as bad as the proponents of any particular bond financing scheme would have the electorate believe at the time of referendum. If ever there was a "now generation," it must include the politicians and businessmen involved in such state and municipal projects.

With a given sum of tax revenues committed to a particular capital improvement for which there is an option to build over the term of the revenue commitment, bond financing yields half in construction and half in interest. The bond financing of highway construction, for example, might yield $100 million in road construction in five years when allowing for the construction time. The issuance of thirty-year bonds to pay for this commonly would require some $75 million to be paid in interest. The real question, therefore, is whether to have $100 million in road construction available in five years through bond financing, or $30 million in five years, $100 million in sixteen years and $180 million in thirty years. If you are in the business of constructing and financing roads the decision is easy. To support your position you might well be tempted to use the argument that if construction is prolonged over such a period, inflation and the resulting rise in costs of construction would diminish the miles of road building from a given amount of revenues.

This argument may well have been correct in past years, but a public policy founded upon a premise that money management in the future will be as bad as it was in the past maligns our form of government and slights our intellect. In effect, it says to the prospective bond buyers that as one of our governing bodies we intend to sell you a bad investment —one which we believe will depreciate substantially in value (purchasing power) over its life and that we will profit at your expense.

Nevertheless, public administrators will always manage to find some need for these bond-financed projects so long as the taxpayers' ability to pay holds out.

The nature of public expenditures is that they lag. Only

117

after the taxpayers' real income declines are they likely to voice strong opposition to increased taxes. Not only are they heard, but subsequent elections will tend to result in the election of people with a more restrained attitude toward public spending. This all takes time, as does the reversal of such a trend—which creates a substantial lag. The depression years of 1930, 1931, and 1932 each witnessed substantial additions to state and local debt. The momentum of the prosperous twenties was halted after three years, however, by the public financial problems and the inability and unwillingness of the taxpayers to assume more public debt.

An occasional reminder, if only a slight one, in the form of a less rapid growth in total income reminds the electorate and public officials to be temperate in governmental affairs. The efforts of the federal government to keep incomes accelerating without regard to consequences have, among other things, caused state and local government officials to become heedless of potential excesses in governmental financing and expenditures.

Perhaps the weakest spot in our economy today is the financial structure of a few of our largest cities. Without going into the social disarrangements caused by welfare incentives, public school management, the accessibility and desirability of the suburbs, immigration, taxation, and so on, these cities are skirting financial disaster. Here we find cities borrowing to meet operating needs as current revenues prove to be inadequate. This parallels our analogy of the drunk who drinks to avoid the hangover. The debt of these cities is great and constitutes a sizable investment of some of the nations largest banks. Default by any of these cities could jeopardize these large banks and many smaller banks. Such a chain of events could very adversely affect the total economy.

FOOTNOTES

1. The Bond Buyer's Municipal Finance Statistics, Vol. 9, May 1970, The Bond Buyer, New York, N.Y.

2. Statistics from the Bureau of Census

3. The Bond Buyer's Municipal Finance Statistics, Vol. 8 p. 8.

4. P.A. Bergquist, "Growth of Municipal Bonds and Purchase by Banks" Commercial and Financial Chronicle, January 3, 1963.

Chapter X

THE CUSTOMER IS ALWAYS RIGHT

It is commonly believed by many that the most important category of debt is that which is generated by the federal government. While the impact based on the size of this debt is essentially equalled by other debts such as the total business debt, or the total consumer debt including mortgage debt, the federal debt has some interesting distinctions. The fact that this debt to some extent can be controlled or manipulated by a relatively small number of people acting in concert (and here we speak of the Congress and the Administration), has attracted much attention. As we have tried to show previously, there is a strong interaction between the development of debts and their various categories. Because the federal debt can be controlled and manipulated, it is understandable why this category has captured the imagination of those who would attempt to steer economic developments.

A more important distinction, however, is the fact that the federal government and its creature the Fed, controls the supply of money and the monetary system of which the federal debt is an integral part. The fact that a small group of individuals can wield such monumental economic power to serve their own short-sighted self interests truly justifies giving this category of debt our most urgent concern.

Funds borrowed by the federal government, like any other borrowings, come ultimately from the savings of individauls and from corporations on behalf of their shareholders and from the expansion of the money supply. If the savings were relatively constant and the money supply did not increase, then added borrowing by the federal government or anyone else would mean a greater competition for existing funds and would result in higher interest rates at least in the short-run. These would rise to a point that would discourage additional borrowing and the quantity of funds available would be equal to the quantity of funds demanded. But because the Federal Reserve System can be enslaved by the federal government to serve its propensities to lean excessively on debt financing, expansion of money has been easily rationalized as being a reasonable alternative.

The fact that the federal debt does not have to be "paid off" and further, that it should not be, has confused many and misled many more. Out of this had developed, not uncommonly, the idea that the correct size of the federal debt is undeterminable, and therefore, exploitable. If its potential size is infinite, and it doesn't have to be reduced, it is reasoned that it is an inexhaustible or nearly inexhaustible source of funds. It is an easy rationalization from this point to the position that increasing the federal debt is more desirable than increasing taxes.

The story of the evolution of our attitudes toward federal debt must span four decades in order to give us a reasonable understanding of how we arrived at the 70's in such confusion. Hopefully, out of an understanding of the mechanics of debt and money, as well as an understanding of human weaknesses and frailty, money and government finances can be managed in a manner which best serves the long-range interests and welfare of the populace of this country and of the world. Critical to the implem'n   c nd economic policies by a government such as ours is very broad support for such policies by the electorate. If the election of public officials is to be determined by very whimsical appraisals of the economic conditions at the moment elections are held, then the government will be condemned to pursue only those policies that are consistent with the very short-term effects on the economy. In politics, failure in the short run is failure in the long run.

In our system the voters are the customers, and the customers are always right. The hope, therefore, for sound long-range economic policies can only be realized if the majority of the voters recognize the difference between unsound economic policies that have spectacular results which coincide with election days and are implemented without regard to the chaos and instability that may follow, and sound long-range policies that by their very nature, cannot be influenced by short two-year intervals of federal elections.

THE GOVERNMENT; ITS INFLATIONS AND ITS DEPRESSIONS

Around the turn of the century, there was much concern about the instability of our monetary system. Up to that time, the money supply in the United States was a product of a fledging banking system, the inflow and outflow of gold, the financing of wars, as well as the production of gold and silver and the politics related thereto. Concern for the monetary panics that occasionally beset the country caused the Federal Reserve System to be created to give "liquidity" to our monetary system through its ability to expand or contract the bank credit, and thereby avoid monetary crises. The theory was that by making the Federal Reserve a quasi-governmental agency and removing it from the direct influence of the Congress and the Administration, it would be removed from political domination and influence. Shortly after its creation, however, it was enlisted to generate the monies to finance World War One. "The large federal government deficits, totaling in all some twenty-three billion dollars, or nearly three-quarters of all expenditures of thirty-two billion dollars from April, 1917 to June, 1919, were financed by explicit borrowing and by money creation. The Federal Reserve became, to all intents and purposes, the bond-selling window of the Treasury, using its monetary powers almost exclusively to that end."[1] This violent expansion of the money supply was accompanied by a rapid rise in wholesale and consumer prices.

From 1915 to 1920, wholesale prices increased over 200%. Ten years later, after a relatively tranquil decade, the Federal Reserve once again, starting in 1929, failed to carry out the intentions of its founders. "From the cyclical peak in August, 1929, to the cyclical trough in March, 1933, the money stock fell by over one-third."[2] The gross economic constriction that accompanied this decline in the quantity of money left the nation and the world in a state of bewilderment. Being generally unaware of these monetary events, people began to grasp at the theories that describe the capitalist system as being "inherently unstable," suffering from "over-production," and being incapable of reinvesting the savings that tend to expand as the nation becomes more prosperous. But out of the economic theories that developed during these depression years grew the concept that the federal government was indeed responsible and accountable for our economic fortunes. These theories magnified the importance of government income and expenditures while underestimating the consequences of overexpanding the money supply. They gained an almost unquestioned universal acceptance which culminated in the highly inflationary government monetary and spending policies of the 1960's. After some years of reasonably stable prices, fear of inflation waned. Fiscal excesses became profitable and popular. By the presidential election of 1964, it was thought that the preservation of booming prosperity was merely a matter of good government—a government that was willing to spend more than its income—its impact on money management being of little consequence.

During the depression days of the thirties, on the other hand, governmental revenues were declining. Normal government operational expenditures plus the implementation of federal projects to alleviate unemployment and raise the level of economic activity brought about substantial deficits. The federal deficits mounted. This combined with the inflow of gold from abroad and caused the money supply to expand. By 1936, it appeared that we were on our way out of the depression. The Federal Reserve, concerned about the "excess reserves" of the banking system, moved to "dry up" these reserves by raising the reserve requirements of the individual banks. "Excess reserves" are the reserves of the individual banks over and above those required by the Federal Reserve for any specific deposits of the bank. They give the individual banks the ability to expand loans and deposits. To rid the banking system of "excess reserves" the Fed needs only to raise the reserve requirements. This was done in late 1936 and early 1937 in a series of steps—a maneuver on the part of the Federal Reserve, which turned out to be one more enormous misjudgment. The "excess reserves" as defined by the Federal Reserve evidently were not excess as defined by individual bankers; the consequence was that the bankers moved to re-establish their excess reserves, thus constricting the money supply and bringing about the recession of 1938. This brought economic activity to the low levels of five years previous to the move. As most economists at that time were not watching monetary aggregates; bewilderment was once again pervasive. After an expansion of the federal debt of some fifty billion dollars, a substantial amount for that time, the economy was still back in the depths of depression in 1938. This was followed by the mobilization for war, and in 1939, 1940 and 1941, federal financing of these defense preparations influenced the money supply expansion and once again the economy returned to prosperity.

The financing of the nearly complete mobilization of the country's resources for the conduct of World War II was the force that caused the federal debt to expand very rapidly. These large federal deficits were met by stimulating individual savings and war bond drives, by increased taxes, and finally, by the monitization of the debt, which is done by selling government securities to the banking system. There is virtually no difference between the process of printing currency and selling bonds to the banking system in order to pay the cost of war or other government expenditures. This caused the money supply to expand 300 percent during the years 1942, 1943, 1944 and 1945. The real inflationary potential of this expansion was enormous. Some of it materialized during the war years in the form of lower quality goods and the "black market," while the bulk of the inflationary potential was merely delayed by price controls and was shifted to the immediate post war years. Prices jumped some fifty percent during this period.

The pain of the monetary excesses and the instability was sufficient to cause the Federal Reserve and the government to pursue reasonably conservative policies and restraint until 1960, when evidently the memory of the post war inflation grew dim.

DELIRIUM TREMENS

Almost a quarter of a century had passed since John Maynard Keynes' General Theory was published in 1936. The income-expenditure theories became more and more refined, complicated, and pervasive. They provided the economist with the confidence of a mathematician and the skill of an astrologer. The theories seemed to provide a reasonable answer for nearly all economic phenomena. With the election of John Kennedy as President, the Keynsian or fiscal economists reigned supreme. The year 1960, in addition to being an election year, was a year of economic recession. John Kennedy chose this economic issue as the most important one upon which to build his presidential campaign. He vowed to end the economic "stagnation" and "to move ahead in the sixties."

Kennedy saw how, when Eisenhower's administration created a surplus in 1960, the economy slid into a recession. The Fed, being guided at that time by interest rates, permitted the money supply to constrict as the federal government ran a surplus and became a supplier of funds. This was a very reasonable occurence because the Fed at that time was not guided by monetary aggregates. Steered by the income-expenditure theories, Kennedy embarked upon a program to sell the nation the idea that the federal debt had shrunk. The argument was that the federal debt had remained essentially the same since the end of World War II and that during the intervening fifteen years, the size of the total economy had grown substantially. Therefore, it was argued, the debt, when related to the total economy, had constricted. From this line of reasoning it was argued that therefore the federal debt could be increased without becoming an added burden to the economy. Thereupon that administration made efforts to increase expenditures and implement a program to cut taxes for the purpose of increasing the federal deficits. This, it was hoped would avoid the terrible prospect of the government operating with a balanced budget. These policies evidently were consistent with Lyndon Johnson's political objectives, since he pursued them zealously.

The tax cut was passed in 1964 and as defense, space, and social expenditures accelerated, so did the federal deficits. The Federal Reserve, chasing interest rates, supplied more and more money to meet the demands of the economic expansion. By 1966, the price indexes had increased to a rate of about 2 percent. Concerned about this, or the rapidly rising stock prices, or whatever, the Fed, in early 1966, embarked upon a policy of monetary restraint. This, as described by J. Allan Rudolph, was to the income-expenditure theories what Christopher Columbus' first voyage was to the flat-world theories. A hypothesis needs only to fail once to be destroyed. Federal deficits were rising and the monetary aggregates were constricting, or, at least, not growing. For the economists in power, money mattered only slightly—federal deficits mattered most. But contrary to these beliefs about the effects of expanding deficits, economic activity slowed, responding to the retarded growth in the money supply. After about nine months of monetary restrictivness in 1966, the economy appeared to be headed into a recession. Subsequently governmental expenditures to finance the accelerated pace of the Vietnam War were rising rapidly. In 1968, a time when there was no "slack" in the economy, a tax increase, in the form of a surtax, was passed. The Board of Governors of the Federal Reserve System being of the persuasion that fiscal matters mattered most, were concerned that the tax increase would be an "over-kill," and so they chose to expand the money supply rapidly in the face of the fiscal restraint. The economy responded to money and not governmental taxing and spending pattern. The "fiscal school" hypothesis failed once again. Hopefully, the experiences of 1966 and 1968 were sufficiently clear to make 1969 the end of an era—the end of the perfect rationale by which the Congress can feel justified in spending more than it taxes without regard for the impact its financing will have on the money supply.

HALF A CENTURY OF STAGGERING

For over half a century, the Federal Reserve has staggered about the streets of money management. The record is one of extremes. From the management of the most severe of depressions to rampant inflations, it has reeled from one side of the interest rate scale to the other. It has leaned to the right and it has leaned to the left. But one of its greatest professed accomplishments has been to "lean into the wind." Observing the Fed's entanglement with interest rates was much like the story of the drunk who walked into a tree. He bounced back, gained his balance, leaned forward and again smashed into the tree. After having repeated this operation three more times, he proclaimed in inebriated futility, "Hopelessly lost in an impenetrable forest." Until 1970 the Fed had defined its monetary policy in terms of interest rates.

It interpreted its efforts in terms of interest rates. Its instructions for the implementation of its policies was in terms of interest rates. If this was not totally frustrating to the Fed, an examination of its record suggests it should have been.

From the middle of 1929 to a time approaching the bank holiday in 1932, the Fed watched the bond markets very orderly rise and of course, the interest rates declined modestly and in orderly fashion. While they watched the tranquility of interest rates, the supply of money shrank to about two-thirds of its previous magnitude. After such a severe and protracted monetary constriction, an acute liquidity crisis developed. As banks and others were forced to sell bonds in efforts to gain liquidity, the markets collapsed and interest rates skyrocketed.

In the forties, the process of supporting treasury financing and treasury bonds kept interest rates at a low level. The stock of money, on the other hand, increased about 200 percent. It had been widely held that easy money meant low interest rates, and tight money meant high interest rates. In the sixties, many interpreted the rising interest rates as being a signal of tight money, while in fact the reverse was true. While the Fed permitted the money supply to grow some fifty to sixty billion dollars in the sixties, interest rates rose to the highest level since prior to the Civil War. The accelerating injection of money into the economy by the Fed increased the aggregate demand similarly, and the interest rates responded accordingly. Dr. Milton Friedman points to the contrasting experiences of Brazil and Switzerland. Brazil, which has followed a very easy monetary policy, one of rapidly expanding its money supply, has had extremely high interest rates; while Switzerland, a country that has pursued a highly restrained monetary policy, has relatively low interest rates. Thus it was the Fed's faulty vision that caused it to fail to provide stability to our economy. The Fed, for years, was satisfied to assume a posture of "leaning against interest rates." If it appeared that the economy was expanding rapidly, it would commonly assume a policy of restricting bank reserves, taking some comfort that this was accomplishing something. This stance generally disregarded the quantity of money and was, as a result, generally ineffective. The forces in the banking system, which without the overriding direction of the Fed, can expand or constrict the quantity of money, generally did not respond well to the Fed's "leaning." The Fed's actions were like a frail man leaning into the force of a hurricane. The Board of Governors of the Federal Reserve System, operating with vague objectives and manifold goals, took on the characteristic common to governmental bodies and agencies throughout the nation, that is, to steer a course that would avoid severe criticism. This constant dodging of any major criticism can lead a governmental body down an infinite number of wrong roads.

With its broad latitude and nebulously defined responsibilities, the Fed's power can be a political threat. The election of 1960 is a good example. Monetary restraint in 1959 and 1960 brought about a recession in that election year. That recession was generally viewed as sufficient to tip the scales, ending eight years of Republican Administration. Had the election been held in a year of prosperity, which of course could have been arranged had the Fed expanded the money supply in late 1959 and early 1960, the prime economic issue that John Kennedy established in the campaign would have been rather ineffectual.

In addition to the Fed's vaguely defined responsibilities and poorly established direction, it has had to serve the Congress much like a mother serves her teen-aged son. He may know that if he has mismanaged his money, turning to his father for additional funds will more likely get him a scolding than money. Whereas, Mom is generally an easy touch. The Congress is equally reticent to put the "bite" on the electorate for its excesses. Its "scoldings" are total rejection at the polls. But the Fed is an easy touch. It has, as a practice, subjugated its objectives to the facilitating of Treasury financing.

BEWARE OF THE VENDORS OF INEBRIATION

We will either abandon the concepts and practices of "printing money" to pay the bills of government or we will be condemned to live in an unstable economy with its inflation, high interest rates, boom and recession. History's lesson is emphatic. Governments that pay their bills with newly created money instead of taxation, inflict inflation upon their economy. Governments in the past actually have printed currency to pay the costs of wars or other governmental functions. As we have pointed out, in this country the same effect is accomplished by the government's selling bonds to the banking system. The result in either case is an expanded money supply. In a money economy such as ours, the expansion of available money at a faster rate than the economy is physically able to expand leads to inflation. And there are very specific limits to the rate at which an economy can expand. The economy may grow as a result of an expansion of the productive capacity through the creation of more capital goods, an increase in the efficiency of capital goods, or an increase in the size or efficiency of the labor force; or, it may grow without any increase in capacity through greater utilization of the existing capacity. But the rate of expansion of any one of these factors is limited. Over the decades our economy has been able to expand at rates ranging roughly between three and four percent. This is a physical boundary within which we as a nation will have to live, like it or not. And that boundary determines the limits of expansion of the money supply without producing inflation.

Inflation diminishes the real return that lenders receive. Without inflation, a three percent interest rate, for example, yields the lender three percent. With a two percent inflation rate, a five percent interest rate yields the lender a net return of three percent. With a five percent inflation rate, an eight percent interest rate yields the lender a net return of three percent. The demand for borrowed funds tends to increase with inflation. In periods of inflation, the prospects of return for borrowers often appear exaggerated. Aggregate demand for goods and services rises and the outlook for new or expanded enterprises appears good. Apart from these conditions, however, borrowers realize that there is a five percent inflation rate and if they can borrow money at four percent, they will be gaining one percent at the expense of the lenders. The demand for such money rises rapidly. Historically, real interest rates, that is the interest rate after it is adjusted for the inflation rate, yields the lender between three and four percent. This means that interest rates tend, perhaps after some lag, to keep pace, or at least rise with the inflation rate of an economy.

Once the inflationary chain of economic events gets started, the pain of adjustment must eventually occur. The more severe and protracted the inflation, the more severe and protracted the adjustment. The adjustment can always be postponed a few years if the government constantly increases the growth rate of the money supply, but only at the cost of a much harsher later adjustment. Rising interest rates, inflation, growing excesses in the stock market and other business ventures will continue toward still greater excesses and maladjustment until the decision is made to halt the acceleration of money or the economy topples under its own weight.

A credit economy such as ours, not only requires borrowers, it requires lenders, whose roles are often downgraded. People commonly view large lending institutions as ruthless exploiters of unfortunate borrowers. They are, however, merely intermediaries or agents of savers. Borrowers often look forward to the prospect of inflation, believing that it will diminish the effective size of their debt and allow them to pay off their creditors with cheap dollars. Such an attitude, however, is a breach of trust. When the borrowers went to the lenders, hat in hand, to seek funds for their own betterment, the lenders cooperated in good faith. Borrowers who support induced inflation seek to break their agreement. An economy that is so dependent upon its lenders should always act to protect those who save. The most direct breach of this sort occurs when Congress, after having borrowed money at rates of two and one-half, three, four and five percent from people acting in good faith, generates an inflation which causes these well-meaning savers to lose money on their investments in government bonds. Not only do rising costs due to inflation decrease the real rate of return on the investment, but the value of the bonds declines.

Failure to levy direct taxes to pay the costs of government has only levied an indirect tax through inflation. The indirect tax burden has, as we have shown, fallen on the savers and persons whose incomes have not risen as much as the rate of inflation. Such taxes are as cruel and as regressive as the mind can conceive.

The Fed, as we have already mentioned, has felt an obligation to finance Congress's extravagant tendencies. Few would contest the assistance of the Federal Reserve System in financing a war for survival. But in other areas perhaps it is the confusion over priorities that caused the Fed to enslave itself to Congress's spending will. Perhaps it is the Fed's historical approach of chasing interest rates that compelled it to indulge our spendthrift government. Whatever the reason, the Fed, as an accomplice, might be compared to the devoted individual who slips his alcoholic friend a fifth of "booze." His devotion outweighs his good judgment. The Congress and its electorate will have to, sooner or later, learn that the growth potential of the economy has very definite limitations, and that the Congress should refrain from exploiting the monetary authorities and the monetary system to pay its bills—for doing so expands money at rates substantially greater than the growth potential of the economy. The cost of government has to be paid for by taxes, either explicit taxes, levied in some rational manner, or implicit taxes that result from inflation and are levied in a grossly irrational manner. Economic stability will not come from the Congress's management of everybody else's affairs; it will come from the Congress's management of its own financial affairs.

FOOTNOTES

1. Milton Friedman, Anna Jacobson Schwartz, A **Monetary History** of the United States 1867-1960, Princeton, Princeton University Press, 1963, p. 216.

2. Ibid p. 299.

Chapter XI

NEVER AGAIN

Man has a compulsion to redesign his environment. This has many manifestations, not the least of which is his compulsion to bend, twist, or, for that matter, totally reform his economic institutions. Many of the schemes conceived for economic revision often overlook certain characteristics of human nature, economics, and politics that are fundamental and unamendable. Commonly, such solutions hinge on human nature, economic law and politicians' behavior being different from what they in fact are. As a result, many programs are ineffective or frequently end up being perverted and applied in some way quite contrary to the intent of the designers. For example, fundamental to human nature affecting all rules applied *to* and applied *by* man is the fact that man's primary inclination is to serve his own short-sighted or short-run self interests first. Those who would deny such motives in themselves have not looked deep enough into their own motivations. People are motivated primarily from within, not from without, and personal needs are pressing and require short-run satisfaction. Schemes that require those applying them and those abiding by them to behave in a manner which is contrary to human nature are doomed. It is only to be expected that planners or administrators of contrived federal programs will act to serve their own interests wherever possible, and when sucessful will move to perpetuate their achievement. If economic institutions are to work, they must be tailored to man and economics as they are, and not to some characteristics which are thought to be desirable.

We have pointed out how our credit institutions evolved

and we have discussed many of the innovations that have been tried. Whenever there appeared to be an economic problem, Congress very frequently adopted measures to liberalize credit. The depression years of the thirties fostered massive revisions in our credit institutions. Excluding the creation of money, credit institutions can do no more than bring savers and borrowers together. The nature of savings and the motivation of savings are such as to suggest that the existing credit institutions have performed their function quite well and that opportunity for solving economic problems by further innovations in our credit institutions is rather limited. Cures for economic ills in the future are not likely to be found in credit innovations.

Capital comes from savings and the creation of money. Economic experience shows us clearly and emphatically that money creation as a suitable source of capital has, in the long run, some very stringent limitations. Aggregate savings, too, are not an unlimited source of funds. The notions of many that economic growth is merely a matter of finding new capital investments and creating credit institutions to supply it will, with or without pain, eventually be dispelled.

In a lifetime we have seen the conventional understanding of credit and investment swing from one extreme to the other. In the thirties, the attitude was spawned which ascribed to the thesis that the economy of the United States was a mature economy, and therefore incapable of investing or reinvesting all of the savings that "were withdrawn from the income stream." It is not uncommon to human nature for individual people to draw conclusions from their current experiences. Being generally unaware of the violent constriction of the quantity of money that occurred in the early thirties, the "insufficient investment," "mature economy," and "secular stagnation" theories drew a wide following. After years of rapid expansion of the money supply which dominated most of the sixties, demand for investment capital became very intense. The conclusion very frequently drawn in the sixties was that the United States has become a "capital short" or "capital deficient" nation, unable to supply the vast needs of businesses, municipalities, states, federal government projects and individuals. Neither of these extreme views is correct. The fact is that there is an equilibrium price (interest rate), at which the funds available for investment and the actual investment will be equal.

Recent schemes to increase the supply of credit to one particular area or another can do so only at the expense of other users of credit. Programs to funnel funds into housing, for example, look reasonable to the people in that industry and those working with housing problems. However, the implementation of their prejudice will be only at a cost of efficiency to the system at large.

The high standard of living and prosperity of the United States is attributable to its enormous capital investment. The funds for this large capital invesment are, in large measure, represented by debt securities. The integrity of debt securities, therefore, must be preserved if this nation is to continue to prosper. Essential to this integrity is an economy that operates without substantial inflation or great significant disruption of income. Inflation has the effect of repudiating debt. It tends to cause interest rates to rise, and thereby disrupts the markets for debt securities.

Frequently it is suggested that there should be controls placed upon credit—that it should be regulated to protect both the borrowers and the lenders. It is proposed that restrictions, limits and guidelines will eliminate bad loans and the resulting loss to the parties involved. Credit arrangements are a result of an agreement between lenders and borrowers. There are judgments involved that assume the existence of certain risks which are agreed upon and entered into between the participants. It is folly to believe that a third party, namely the government, should inject itself into these agreements. A stable economic environment, on the other hand, does a great deal toward avoiding the misjudgments and the misfortunes associated with bad loans. Nothing was more disruptive in our credit structure than the pre-

137

cipitous restriction of the money supply in the years 1930, 1931 and 1932. Given a reasonably stable business climate, borrowers and lenders can meet and make reasonably sound judgments which will result in their mutual benefit.

MONEY—THE CATALYST

Our obsession with credit and credit institutions since the depression of the thirties led many to believe that money wasn't very important. Until the last half of the sixties, little importance was given to money. Through the banking system, money was made the slave of our credit needs, particularly those of the federal government.

Many people still believe that the dollar ultimately derives its value from gold and our gold reserves. This really isn't the case, however. The dollar derives its value from the productive capability of our country. Its ability to be exchanged for this productivity, both domestically and abroad, is what really gives the dollar value. Recognizing again that the American economy grows at an annual rate of about three or four percent, the "basis of value" of the dollar, therefore grows at three or four percent annually. Substantial deviation from that rate of growth on the part of the money stock will only cause changes in prices. For example, if the economy, which grows at three to four percent, is the basis of value of the dollar, and the number of dollars increases at the rate of fifty or sixty percent, then it would be only reasonable to assume that the larger number of dollars chasing this limited total production would become worth less. Regardless of how we might wish it to be different, the fact is that the economy grows at this rate and that money will have to be confined to grow at a similar rate if the economy is to operate without inflation or deflation. The evidence suggests that it is unthinkable that an economy can enjoy stable growth and at the same time have a grossly unstable growth rate in its money supply.

138

This is not to suggest that a stable growth rate in the money supply means total stability in the economy. It does suggest, however, that the economy would enjoy far greater stability than we have witnessed in the past. In a system such as ours, which is so responsive to the demands of the consumer, there is a constant reallocation of the productive resources. New businesses are formed and old businesses that no longer serve the desires of the consumer are dismantled or rearranged. This process of constant adjustment to the whims of the consumer has inherent potential for misjudgments by businessmen trying to anticipate and forecast these changing demands. These over-estimations and misjudgments will always cause fluctuation in the level of economic activity. Expectations on the part of consumers will, from time to time, change. The longer any one trend is in force, the more warped the expectations and projections become, by both the businessman and the consumer. Booms or expansions of long duration distort predictions and speculation in stock or land heightens. While we can always expect fluctuations in the level of business activity as long as we enjoy the fruits of a free economy, these fluctuations need not be as extreme as we have witnessed in the past—swinging from the depths of depression of the thirties to the excesses of inflation and inflationary boom of the sixties. As personal moderation can enable a person to avoid the emotional peaks of elation and troughs of deep depression, moderation in monetary policy avoids the peaks of inflationary boom and the depths of economic depression.

THE ROLE OF GOVERNMENT

We have become insufficiently creative in dealing with our economic problems. Almost single-mindedly we turn to the federal government to solve our problems. This approach has virtually precluded any search for solutions that do not involve the federal government. It constantly threatens our hopes for economic stability, growth of productivity—and our freedom. The experiences in this country and the experiences of Socialistic countries offer little hope that the most desirable solution of economic problems can be achieved through the central government. The remarkable feats of the private enterprise system have been accomplished in an environment which motivates self-serving people and businesses to meet the needs, desires, and whims of the consumer.

Some of our citizens do not have sufficient abilities, talent, or capital assets to enjoy even a sustaining allotment of goods and services. The cause of their insufficient endowment is more properly a concern of the sociologists than the economists. The best economic solution at this stage is to provide them with cash, neither in such great amount nor in such a manner as to stifle incentive but sufficient to let the private enterprise system respond to their needs as they themselves conceive them. This would avoid the intervention of special interests who would have government channel such funds through them first—thus serving *their* interests while much of the time they disregard the interests of the supposed beneficiaries. (We see this in the construction industry in the building of "low rent" housing and in the farm industry in its distribution of commodity foods.) It would circumvent the egotistical do-gooders who are convinced that they know best and that they should direct what and how aid-recipients consume. With payments more uniform throughout the country, these recipients could move about rather than gravitate to the highest cost-of-living areas—the cities—which ironically have been paying vast sums to acquire and retain these indigents. Such a nationwide system of cash disbursements on an impersonal basis, while not perfect, would be far better than the present perverting, distorting, degrading and inefficient welfare system that is torturing us socially and strangling us financially.

Milton Friedman admonishes, "the 'new liberal' recognizes

that government has an important role to play, but is suspicious of assigning to government any functions that can be performed through the market, both because this substitutes coercion for voluntary cooperation in the area in question and because, by giving government an increased role, it threatens freedom in other areas."[1]

During the four decades following the great monetary constriction of the early thirties, government has become more and more accountable in the minds of the public for the level of business activity. This accountability for recessions undoubtedly led Lyndon Johnson in 1967, to a path that promoted a rapid expansion of the money supply through which he aborted a recession that would have undoubtedly occurred during his administration in 1967. Richard Nixon could have chosen the same course. Through a continuation of an increasing rate of expansion of the money supply, he, too, could have delayed an economic adjustment for another four years. Such a delayed adjustment would have been more severe and protracted than the 1969-70 experience, just as the experience of 1969-70 was more severe and protracted than an adjustment in 1967 would have been. This leads us to the conclusion that when government tries to control the level of business activity, the system works in such a way as to produce decisions that are grossly unsound in the long run, but quite suitable in a political sense, to the short run. Short run accountability on the part of government is not compatible with the long-term growth and well-being of our economy.

Economic growth potential is infinite. To pursue policies that race us down a road to infinity so fast as to insure that the runners will stumble and fall from exhaustion is incredible. It is not uncommon, however, to hear a politician suggest essentially the same policies with respect to economic growth. They have frequently been heard to say that the economy has not been growing fast enough, and that it needs stimulation—which, of course, their election will insure.

While the stimulants may have new names, they have for centuries been the same—through one means or another, expansion of the money supply.

If the recession "hangover" has not created enough anguish to beget an attitude of reform, and a swearing off of the economic booze—money—then another hangover is just down the road.

FOOTNOTES

1. Milton Friedman, A **Program for Monetary Stability**, p. 4, Fordham University Press, NYC, 1960.